Praise

"*A remarkable book filled with* [...] [...] *a viable success formula anyon* [...] *had a better head for business,* [...] *...w Davis.*"

—Jay Baer, President of Convince & Convert and author of
Hug Your Haters

"*This book will inspire anyone who has ever wanted to build a community. Andrew spells it out: Leaders make our towns and cities and if you lead, you can define a community for generations to come. This is a book about leadership and citizenship, two of the most undervalued human qualities. It's a must-read for anyone who cares about the future of their community.*"

—Bryan Welch, CEO, B the Change Media. Author of
"Beautiful and Abundant: Building the World We Want."

"*Andrew Davis is at it again bringing his amazing insight and unique perspective into making businesses grow, prosper and contribute to building thriving communities. Town Inc. is a roadmap for how to* bring your visionary business leadership to building a business and nurturing your own community."

—Michael Brenner, Founder and CEO, Marketing Insider
Group

"*If America is truly the Land of Opportunity, "Town Inc." provides the directions to put your town on the map.*"

—Buddy Scalera, Author, Speaker. Senior Director of
Content Strategy at The Medicines Company.

"*If your ailing town wants to create location envy, learn the benefits of high unemployment or see how a shoe polish brand is helping revive Detroit, then read Town Inc. before it's too late.*"

—Josh Miles, National branding speaker, principal
of Miles Herndon, and author of Bold Brand

TOWN INC.

Grow Your Business.
Save Your Town.
Leave Your Legacy.

ANDREW M. DAVIS

Andrew M. Davis
Monumental Shift
27 Russell St.
Charlestown, Massachusetts 02129
617.286.4009
Elizabeth@monumentalshift.com
www.townincbook.com
Cover design and interior layout by www.pearcreative.ca

Ordering Information:
Quantity sales. Special discounts are available on quantity purchases by corporations, associations, and others. For details, contact Elizabeth Davis at 617.286.4009,

Town Inc / Andrew M. Davis. —1st ed.
ISBN 978-0-9966889-0-1

For Elizabeth,
Who staked her claim to my heart.

CONTENTS

INTRODUCTION
True American Visionaries

Town Inc. is the modern-day story of true American visionaries. These exceptional entrepreneurial leaders do more than cultivate their own businesses. They proactively define the place – the town – in which they build their businesses. These leaders are inextricably linked to the locations they've chosen to live and work. They rise to become the exemplars of entire industries. They turn quiet villages into thriving towns and idle towns into busy cities. These wise leaders actively create an unforgettable legacy.

In the same way that Henry Ford is synonymous with Detroit, Andrew Carnegie transformed Pittsburgh or even Bill Hewlett and Dave Packard defined Silicon Valley, today's wise visionaries transform the towns where they work into a powerful asset.

That asset then attracts an amazing talent pool, builds the infrastructure required to grow, and fosters a support system that drives exponential success for everyone.

Three years ago, I set out to understand why some American towns and cities are booming while others are bust. I crisscrossed the nation visiting 50 cities, towns, and neighborhoods looking for an answer. I expected to uncover innovative economic development models that fostered growth. I imagined I might discover smart tax incentives or development zones that could be replicated to save America's dying towns. But that's not what I found.

My journey revealed something much more enlightening and even more accessible:

The difference between prosperity and economic struggle comes down to one simple thing: a visionary business leader or leaders relentlessly fostering an audacious claim.

Those visionaries make a claim larger than their business, even larger than their town. Tomorrow's Fords and Hewlett Packards are being built right now in towns you've never heard of by visionaries you've never met. These leaders are accelerating the growth of their businesses by marketing their town. They're staking their claim. And they are transforming America, one town at a time.

Town Inc. is about those people. It's about the businesses they've built, the towns they've saved, and the legacy they're creating. It's about the transformative power of an audacious claim. A claim anyone, especially you, can foster.

In the chapters that follow, we will uncover exactly why your business' growth is intricately linked to the place in which you locate. We'll visit **Warsaw, Indiana: The Orthopedic Capital of the World**, to learn how one town attracts young dreamers and smart innovators using a powerful emotional concept called location-envy.

We'll explore towns such as:

- **Batavia, New York: The Greek Yogurt Capital of the World**

- **Muscle Shoals, Alabama: The Hit Record Capital of the World**

- **Hamilton, Missouri: The Quick Quilting Capital of the World**

- **Elkhart, Indiana: The RV Capital of the World**

- And a dozen more...

We'll then learn how to create a sense of place. We'll introduce you to the three fundamental elements that support a successful claim: micro-clustering, origin stories, and true visionaries.

I'll take you to **Arcata, California, The Cannabis Capital of the World** where we'll see how the right kind of claim can transform pessimism into optimism. We'll visit the **World's Largest Ball of Paint in Alexandria, Indiana,** to find out how to reinstate a sense of community pride. Along the way, we'll go to **Greensburg, Kansas** to look at how a simple claim can even unify a politically divided community. We'll take you inside of these communities to pinpoint the simple strategy smart visionaries use to grow, get, and keep new dreamers and innovators.

The point of all of this is to answer two simple questions:

- Why are some American towns booming while others are bust?

- What can you do to spark and foster sustainable growth for your business and your town?

The Tale of Two Towns
The $2.9 Billion Difference

In January of 2015, Professor Paul Fombelle of Northeastern University in Boston, Massachusetts enlisted the help of two students to help quantify the difference between the cities and towns who follow the methodologies in Town INC and those that do not. What we found is staggering.

Throughout this book, you'll find excerpts from The Tale of Two Towns research conducted by Sahil Hundal and Matthew Gefen.

Our investigation spanned twenty-seven pairs of towns (fifty-four towns in total.) Each pair consisted of one town who adhered to the Town INC formula and an "equivalent" town without a recipe for success. (Each town equivalent chosen for its demographic and geographic relevancy.)

The bottom line: on average, the difference between towns who follow the prescription in this book and those that don't is an astonishing $2.9 billion pumping into their economy.

For an in-depth look at the data and the results of our research visit: www.townincbook.com/taleof2towns

CHAPTER ONE
An Audacious Claim

As I explored America's contemporary boomtowns, I noticed one amazing shared attribute: they all stake their claim as a 'capital of the world.' Could something so simple be so powerful? Could the key to unlocking unparalleled success be as easy as filling in a blank? As in, "My town is the _____ Capital of the World!" On the surface it might appear so.

What do I mean?

- Nashville, Tennessee, is the Country Music Capital of the World.

- Hollywood, California, is the Entertainment Capital of the world.

- Hartford, Connecticut, is the Insurance Capital of the World.

- Silicon Valley is the Technology Capital of the World.

- Houston, Texas is the Energy Capital of the World.

All of these places have staked their claim. These places are known for something remarkable, instead of nothing memorable.

If you want to make it in country music, there's only one place in the world to be. A startup in Silicon Valley is seemingly more credible than a startup based anywhere else in the world. If you want access to the best insurance personnel in the world, Hartford has them. That's the power of a simple claim: It makes a specific set of people and businesses wonder why they're not in your town.

An audacious claim sparks unparalleled growth by simplifying your image and defining your role in the world's economy.

Staking your claim sounds elegantly simple, doesn't it? But, I know what you're thinking. It can't be that easy.

You're right. Staking your claim isn't as simple as slapping a moniker on the "welcome to town" sign and waiting for the world to show up.

These audacious claims are powerful. But why? To be audacious your town's claim must attract the innovators and the dreamers. An innovator like Dr. Lon Weiner.

Attracting The Innovators

Dr. Lon Weiner is an orthopedic surgeon in Red Bank, New Jersey, an hour south of New York City. He's also an inventor. In his day-to-day work in the operating room, Dr. Weiner developed a series of new ideas for orthopedic products. Now, all he needed was a way to bring these products to market. In 2009, Dr. Weiner and a fellow surgeon/inventor, Dr. Stuart Katchis, decided to start a new company called Nextremity Solutions and they headquartered it right there in Red Bank.

The company's goal was to help other orthopedic surgeons turn their innovations into marketable products, and it was working. Nextremity Solutions was successful in Red Bank.

But in 2013, after a private-equity investment of $10 million Nextremity Solutions picked up their executive offices and the fifteen full-time employees on staff and moved them to a little town an hour west of Fort Wayne, Indiana on rural route 30 in northern Indiana called Warsaw.

Why Warsaw?

"The move to Warsaw, according to CFO Frank Patton, was not only because it has the right address for the orthopedic industry, but because it also has the orthopedic talent pool needed to grow the company." [1]

The right address for the orthopedic industry? The talent pool needed to grow the company? What could Warsaw, Indiana,

---

[1]   Press Release, September 4, 2013, "Ortho Company Moving Headquarters to Warsaw," Ink-Free News

possibly have to offer that Red Bank can't? What resources and talent could convince a $10 million dollar start-up to pack up a truck, rent new office space, buy new houses, and move their staff 720 miles to a town of 13,000 people without an international airport?

You see, three of the five largest orthopedic manufacturing companies in the world are based in Warsaw, Indiana. The Nextremity Solutions team believes that their chances of success in Warsaw are better than Red Bank or New York or San Francisco or anywhere else in the world.

How do we do what Warsaw, Indiana has done? How do we become so appealing, so attractive, that businesses from around the globe start to wonder if they wouldn't be more successful in our Town?

We stake our claim.

Warsaw is an economic oasis in the middle of the American rust belt and they've done it by staking their claim as the Orthopedic Capital of the World.™ But it's not enough to just attract the innovators. You must attract the dreamers, too. Dreamers such as Billy Currington.

Attracting The Dreamers

We live in a world where you can work anywhere.

Employees telecommute and teleconference. Companies outsource to an army of stay-at-home employees. It is easier and easier to call, email, and Skype into the office. Manufacturers are offshoring their operations. Entire organizations, sometimes with hundreds of employees, have no physical space. They use virtual offices. Entrepreneurs and consultants pack coffee shops as they work on their mobile devices. Today's technology allows you to connect with teams across continents. Suddenly, time zones wither away.

Many people believe that where you do your work won't matter in the future.

We have to make it matter. If you can work from anywhere, why settle down in our city?

For years, Billy Currington told his classmates that he was going to college to play football. But three weeks after he graduated from high school near Savannah, Georgia he packed up and headed to Nashville. It was 1992, and his family couldn't comprehend the swift shift in direction. But they were supportive when Billy hit the highway to pursue his dream of becoming a country music star.

Twenty-two years after Billy Currington left Georgia, he's a country music star and the proud recipient of a Country Music Television award and a Grammy nomination. Billy still lives in Nashville.

In 2006, George Sloan packed up his '98 Honda Accord for the cross-country trek to Los Angeles. He had $1,200 in his bank account ($3,800 less than he thought he needed) and a deep desire to become a screenwriter. As he bid his family farewell he asked himself one last time:

"Aside from film and television, is there anything else I can see doing with my life?"

"No." He thought.

With Boston in his rearview mirror George Sloan was on his way to Hollywood.

Eight years later, George Sloan was a scriptwriter for the hit television show, How I Met Your Mother, and he still lives in Los Angeles.

The summer after her junior year of high school, Rebecca Feick attended a biomedical engineering class at the University of Tennessee. She loved it. *"[Biomedical engineering allows me to] engage my natural bent towards math, science, and problem solving while allowing me to make a direct impact in bettering people's quality of life," Feick says.*[2] In the fall of 2011, Rebecca enrolled in Purdue University's Biomedical Engineering program and she's scheduled to graduate in the class of 2015. What's her plan after graduation? *"I plan on pursuing a job in the orthopedic industry as a development or quality engineer."*

Where's she planning on finding this dream job? Warsaw, Indiana, where she's already spent three semesters as a co-op student at Zimmer Orthopedics, one of the largest orthopedic manufacturing firms in the world.

Every year, millions of people like Chad, George, and Rebecca pack up their stuff and hit the road to pursue their dreams. **Where do dreamers move? Anywhere they believe that their chance of success is the best it can possibly be.**

---

2   Purdue University Website, Weldon School of Biomedical Engineering, Ambassadors www.eng.purdue.edu/jump/ad5002

Would Billy have become a country star if he'd never left Georgia? Possibly. Would George be writing for a hit sitcom if he hadn't fled suburban Boston? Perhaps. Could Rebecca find a job in the orthopedic industry back home in Nashville? We'll never know.

If we're going to infuse new revenue into our towns and see our businesses grow, how do we do what Hollywood, Nashville, Houston, and Warsaw have done? How do we attract the dreamers?

- George Sloan moved to Hollywood because it's the Entertainment Capital of the World.

- Billy Currington chose to live in Nashville because it's the Country Music Capital of the World.

- Rebecca Feick is moving to Warsaw, Indiana, because it's the Orthopedic Capital of the World.

How do we attract the dreamers? We stake our claim.

CHAPTER TWO
The Power of Location-Envy

You see, a claim so big, so audacious, creates an emotional connection in the minds of the dreamers and the innovators. It conjures up a powerful image of success tied directly to the place that proclaims it. **A claim creates location-envy: the emotional belief that one's success is defined by the location of one's work.**

We've been taught that envy is bad. (It <u>is</u> one of the seven deadly sins.) But location-envy is benign. The envy we've been encouraged to avoid is destructive. Location-envy is constructive. It's a unifying force, an amazing source of pride, a tremendous motivator, and — most importantly —a powerful emotion.

The rise of New York as the Investment Banking Capital of the World and the positioning of Warsaw, Indiana, as the Orthopedic

Capital of the World™ are textbook examples of location-envy in action. Location-envy only occurs when one believes that their own community cannot deliver the success that they can achieve elsewhere. Location-envy only exists when one believes their success is defined by the place they do business.

If we're to rebuild our slice of America, we must help create a deep-seated desire in the minds of others to move to our town. We must make people believe that there is no place better-suited to build their business and realize their potential than our city. We must manufacture location-envy in the minds of the business leaders, the innovators, and the dreamers we want to attract.

You don't need charts and graphs or stats and spreadsheets to get the right businesses to move to your town. You need to make them envious. You need to help them believe that until they move to our town they will be unable to tap the secrets of our success.

Location-envy is quite simply the emotional difference between boom and bust.

Look back at the reasons Nextremity Solutions moved to Warsaw: "It has the right address for the orthopedic industry...". Remember why Rebecca Feick is making the same move: to pursue her dream of becoming a development engineer in the orthopedic industry. These aren't logical reasons (Although, as you'll learn a town with a claim has the data to back it up.) They're emotional decisions.

Neurologist Donald Calne sums up exactly why location-envy works: **"The essential difference between emotion and reason is that emotion leads to action while reason leads to conclusions."** Emotion leads to action. Reason leads to conclusions. Location-envy appeals to the emotional side of our brains. Towns and cities who foster a claim inspire people to move by tapping into an irrational, emotional appeal and a deep-seated desire to be more successful tomorrow than they are today.

Location-envy creates a connection between the place we've built our businesses and the success we've seen. It creates a connotation, a feeling about our town that connects our desire for success with a specific place in the world. These kinds of emotional connections and connotations are sticky. Not only do they appeal to those in the industry, they're easy to remember. A great claim is simple to pass on.

A claim, such as The Orthopedic Capital of the World™, isn't imaginary. It's a badge of honor. A valid claim is earned. A powerful claim is based on the existing accomplishments of the business already being done in town. A great claim is rooted in your business and its prosperity.

Long before Warsaw trademarked their claim (yes, they want to protect their claim so fervently that they have trademarked it) a guy named Revra DePuy set up shop in the Hayes Hotel in their dusty little downtown.

A History of Success

It was 1895 and Revra DePuy realized that fractured bones would more effectively heal if set in a fiber splint instead of traditional wooden staves commonly used in that era. In a cramped downtown hotel room Revra DePuy became the world's first orthopedic manufacturer.

In 1926, one of DePuy's fiber splint salesmen recognized an opportunity to expand the business. Justin Zimmer believed that adding aluminum splints to the DePuy product line would drive even more revenue. When DePuy's widow refused to allow Justin to expand the product line and buy a share in the company, Mr. Zimmer struck out on his own. By the end of the year, Warsaw was home to two orthopedic manufacturers.

Today, these two companies alone employ more than 12,000 employees around the world. They sell their products in over 100 countries and generate billions of dollars in annual revenue. Zimmer wasn't the last orthopedic manufacturer to set up shop in Warsaw. Biomet, Paragon, Symmetry, and Medtronic are just a few of the companies that have laid down their roots in the Orthopedic Capital'.

Revra DePuy started a century of economic growth in a small Indiana town that now anchors an entire industry. The global orthopedic market is worth $38 billion dollars and one-third of that is based in Warsaw. Orthopedic-related businesses account for $11 billion dollars in annual revenue for this unassuming little town. And in Kosciusko County (where Warsaw sits) the industry is responsible for 13,000 jobs.

This economic activity isn't just orthopedic device manufacturing. Warsaw has attracted some of the world's best scientists and researchers with their simple claim. So much research and development activity happens in Warsaw that it could actually also lay claim to the Patent Capital of the World. The average patenting rate in the United States is five per 10,000 people. In Warsaw it's 32. Warsaw residents file six times more patents every year than anywhere else in the country.

Today, "the Warsaw, Indiana, orthopedic device cluster is one of the most concentrated centers of economic activity anywhere in the United States."[3]

If you're in the orthopedic industry and you're not in Warsaw, you're not where orthopedic innovation happens. And, inevitably, you will ask yourself why not?

Instead of trying to convince dreamers and innovators to move to Warsaw, they've captured the imagination of an entire industry and flipped the question on its head. If you want to be in Orthopedics why not be in Warsaw?

The question we want the world to be asking about our cities and towns is: "Why shouldn't I move my business there?"

In town after town, I heard the same kinds of stories. Instead of trying to attract non-native businesses to town, one specific company and their visionary leader, set the foundation for a claim. In every single case an existing success story (sometimes two) would be repeated over and over. Successful towns don't attempt to lure new businesses to town. They capitalize on the accomplishments of the businesses already there. Successful towns leverage your success to build the next generation. A little later on I'll reveal the simple three-step process visionaries use to build their economies from the inside out.

I should point out that your town's history of success doesn't have to be centuries old. In subsequent chapters, we'll see examples

---

3   BioCrossroads Report, Warsaw, Indiana Orthopedic Capital of the World, An Overview, analysis, and blueprint, for future industry and community growth, September, 2009

of towns and cities that have leveraged brand new local success stories to stake their claim. But, you must remember that every boom town I visited leveraged a local success story to fuel the future.

Warsaw hasn't just rested on their orthopedic laurels to stake their claim. They actively market their success as The Orthopedic Capital of the World™ and they've taken an approach I haven't seen anywhere else in the world. In Warsaw, it's not just the industry that fuels the town. The town fuels the industry.

Marketing Your Success

Your town doesn't have an economic development problem, you have a communications crisis. You have a marketing problem.

Towns have watered down their value to the nation by using all sorts of economic development buzzwords. Political jargon has homogenized our cities. We describe our towns and neighborhoods as "premiere business destinations." We promote our workforce as "motivated, educated and diverse." We showcase our infrastructure as "high-tech." We all tout a "high quality of life" for our residents.

Homogeneity is the enemy of growth.

By positioning our towns for everyone, we've attracted no one.

Every town in our great nation is unique. It might be a premiere business destination, but for whom exactly? We might have an educated and motivated workforce, but what kind of education do they have and what are they motivated to do? Your town's quality of life might be wonderful, but it's not for everyone. Who exactly are you trying to attract? Let's focus on attracting the right businesses and people to invest in our communities. Your town isn't for anyone, but it is for someone. We've got to ask ourselves "why are we here?"

Ironically, you tell me your town is unique, but you don't show me how. If your town offers the same things as every other town in the country, positioned the same way as everyone else, you're not unique at all. Our tax incentives look the same. Our workforce development plan sounds the same. Our infrastructure investments, technology hubs, sustainable initiatives, all sound the same. It's time to be different. It's time to sound different. It's time to look different.

Warsaw, Indiana, is different.

Go to Warsaw, Indiana's website and take a look at their "Business page." (www.warsaw.in.gov) Thirty-four words into the description of their town you'll find this:

> "Beneath the small-town ambiance hums an $11 billion engine, a highly profitable and fast-growing global orthopedics industry that sets this quiet Northern Indiana community apart from most other communities across the state–and the country."[4]

The entire city has embraced their claim as the Orthopedic Capital of the World™ and they evangelize that message wherever and whenever they can. In Warsaw, a separate non-profit, called

---

4   Warsaw.in.gov, Lilly Endowment 2010 Annual Report - article features Warsaw, Building on strength: Initiative Spotlights "World's Orthopedic Capital" in Indiana

OrthoWorx, has taken the reigns with one simple mission: "ensuring The Orthopedic Capital of the World remains right here in the Warsaw area."[5]

OrthoWorx, initially funded by a grant in 2009, has grown into exactly the kind of collaborative effort required to make a community work and grow. A community is a group of people, who share common attitudes, interests, and goals, who get together in the same place. OrthoWorx has assembled a powerful board of orthopedic manufacturers, life science partners, and regional stakeholders who all share a common goal: ensure the region reaps the social and economic benefits from its position as the Orthopedic Capital of the World.

"We started to wonder, 'who's getting up every day asking themselves how can we expand and maintain our foothold as the orthopedic capital of the world?'" says OrthoWorx executive director, Brad Bishop. *"That's why we founded OrthoWorx. It's taken us 100 years to get here. We want to see the industry grow here for the next 100 years,"* he adds. And that's exactly what they're focused on.

In the Orthopedic Capital of the World they've leveraged their claim to motivate nearby educational institutions like Purdue, Notre Dame, and half-a-dozen others to develop orthopedic focused programming and training assistance. OrthoWorx has spearheaded the development of new transportation and logistics initiatives to keep pace with the needs of their specific cluster. They even invest time and energy in enhancing community pride by upgrading parks, walking trails, even City Hall.

---

5   www.OrthoWoxIndiana.com About us Page

Warsaw isn't for everyone. But it _is_ for someone. It's built for orthopedic dreamers and innovators and they actively maintain and market their claim every single day.

But why spend all this time attracting dreamers and innovators if they've already built a booming economy? Warsaw is working to combat one of the biggest problems facing American towns and businesses today: revenue recycling.

Stop Revenue Recycling

We are revenue recycling masters.

The grocery store clerk spends their money at the local gas station. The gas station attendant gets their haircut at the local barber. The barber gets their teeth cleaned at the dentist down the street. The local dentist goes back to the grocery store. And the cycle continues. This is revenue recycling.

Without an infusion of outside revenue our business and our towns won't grow. They can't grow. Which means we have three options:

1. Foster, encourage, and stimulate the growth of businesses that manufacture products or provide services that are consumed outside of our communities.

2. Attract a steady stream of new businesses and people to our neighborhood to infuse cash into our local economy.

3. Do both. Create an economy where we're known for providing specific goods or services worldwide on such

a scale that it attracts a steady stream of outsiders to our community.

Any of these three strategies breaks the revenue recycling chain. Strategies like these infuse new (and much needed) revenue into our economies and grows our businesses. Whether you own the local pizza place, a marketing agency or an industrial manufacturing firm, you must focus on fresh revenue infusion if you, and your town, are to grow.

Staking our claim powers this growth. A great claim combats revenue recycling.

Now it's time for you to stake your claim.

The Tale of Two Towns
28 Miles and $628 MM Away

Just 28 miles down the road from Warsaw, Indiana is the town of Plymouth. Manufacturer shipments from a town can be used determine how heavily the city relies on revenue recycling. While the populations of Warsaw and Plymouth are similar (14,000 versus 11,000 respectively,) Warsaw, Indiana generates 69% more revenue (about $628MM more) than the town of Plymouth by exporting goods.

To learn more about the Tale of Two Towns research go to www.townincbook.com/taleof2towns.

CHAPTER THREE
Stake Your Claim

True American visionaries stake their claim. And, they start by identifying the businesses in town that are already successful. This means that if you're going to stake your claim you must start by looking at the businesses already here. These success stories set a foundation for your future success. You need to find your Revra DePuy.

In my nationwide travels I asked hundreds of people the same two questions.

- First, I asked people what their town was known for. I'd listen intently to the answer.

- Then, I'd ask them to fill in this blank: "My town is the _____ capital of the world." What I found was amazing.

At a convention in Orlando I happened to sit at a table with a wonderful gentleman from Fargo, North Dakota. When I asked him what Fargo was known for he thought for a few seconds and then responded:

"We have a really active technology community. It's like a little Silicon Valley. They're doing really neat stuff."

I nodded, and then asked him my typical follow-up question:

"If you had to fill in the blank in the following sentence what would it be? Fargo, North Dakota is the _____ capital of the world."

Without skipping a beat he said, *"Oh, that's easy. Fargo, North Dakota, is the Sugar Beet Capital of the World."*

What followed was a fifteen-minute conversation about sugar beets. I learned what they are (a giant white beet) and what they're used for (the extracted sugar is used in tons of energy drinks.) But most importantly, I quickly learned that American Crystal is one of the largest suppliers of refined sugar in the nation. I also learned that one of the reasons sugar beets fare so well in North Dakota is because of the fertile, north-flowing Red River.

I'll forever think of Fargo, North Dakota, as the Sugar Beet Capital of the World.

This happened over and over again. When I asked people what their town is known for I'd get vague answers. However, as soon as I asked them to fill in the blank, I received amazingly interesting, intriguing and sticky responses. The conversations that resulted revealed the existing success stories ready to be tapped.

Now it's your turn: I want you to start by trying to fill in the blank: my town is the _____ capital of the world.

If you can't think of how to fill in the blank, start listing all the successful businesses in your neighborhood. Go for a drive around the city. Stop into the office buildings and look at the corporate directory in the lobby. What do these companies do? Why are they here?

It's not unreasonable to believe that Fargo, North Dakota could turn the Sugar Beet Capital of the World into the Energy Drink Capital of the World. All it takes is one fledgling success story to shape an entirely new and exciting vision for an entire city. (In a few chapters, I'll help you uncover the vast difference in economic impact between the Sugar Beet Capital and the Energy Drink Capital.)

Start looking for your Revra DePuy. And while you're at it, look for claims that target a micro-cluster, have a compelling origin story, and are spearheaded by a visionary. These are the three critical elements of a successful claim. A successful claim is all designed to own a corner of your mind.

Own a Corner of Their Mind

Towns that leverage a simple, original claim do something special every time it's told. They own a small corner of the listener's mind. Claims, as big as Hollywood's and as small as Warsaw's, work. Why?

Claims are easy to remember and to re-tell. More importantly, the more it's told the more we believe it to be true. The more often our claim circulates, the more often we'll actually spark an innovator or a dreamer to move to our town. (That's why you must harness media momentum which we'll dissect later on.)

Simple, smart, claims set a trigger in our minds. A trigger is a prompt that aligns a connection between two things in our minds. For example, anytime you meet someone in the orthopedic business from now on, you'll remember that Warsaw is the Orthopedic Capital of the World™. Just as when you meet someone who lives in Hollywood you immediately assume they must be in the entertainment business.

Claims are the most powerful type of location-based triggers connecting a place to a profession or an entire industry in an elegantly memorable statement.

A claim alone is not enough. In fact, to set and retain a memorable trigger your claim must be supported by three essential elements:

1. An origin story

2. A cornerstone for a cluster

3. A visionary

Let's unpack each of these three elements and the three laws that govern your ability to create a successful claim. Because, when used wisely, these three elements help create a sense of place.

CHAPTER FOUR
The Laws of Attraction

Sense of Place

An audacious claim has the power to immediately create a sense of place. It simplifies your message and empowers the rest of world to paint their own picture of what your town looks like. What it feels like. What businesses drive your economic engine? A claim even helps us imagine who lives in your town and what kind of lifestyle they live. Ironically, psychiatrists, sociologists, cartographers, even social scientists, have spent decades trying to determine what goes into creating a sense of place.

So, what exactly is a sense of place? Here's a nice definition:

Sense of place is a way of describing the emotional relationship that an individual has with a particular area. It is a value-laden concept that encapsulates a person's feelings, perceptions, attitudes and behavior towards a place.[6]

There you go: a sense of place "encapsulates" the connotations, perceptions, and even the behaviors towards a place. Unfortunately, many of the towns and cities I visited on my great American journey have lost their sense of place. I invite you to take any exit off the interstate to visit a typical town you've never been to before. You'll almost certainly find that it's hard to tell this town from the next. They look the same. They feel the same. They even sound the same when one describes them. Remember, **homogeneity is the enemy of growth.**

Claims like **The Orthopedic Capital of the World™** or the **Sugar Beet Capital of the World,** immediately differentiate our towns, they begin to create a sense of place. They start to foster location-envy (in the right audience's mind). But a great claim is only a gateway to creating and communicating a unique sense of place. It invites the rest of the world to learn more. To ask questions. It empowers us to paint a more intricate and meaningful mental image of our town.

In order to effectively capitalize on your claim and build on the connotations and perceptions a claim begins to create, it must adhere to three laws:

1. The Law of The Origin Story

2. The Law of The Cornerstone

---

6   Shamai S 1991, Geoforum, vol. 22, pp. 347-58.

3. The Law of The Visionary

These three laws offer us a way to manufacture a sense of place. They arm us with the tools we need to create location-envy so powerful it will attract the innovators and the dreamers. But before we look at these laws in detail, let's explore the ways in which we usually describe our towns and why they don't allow us to carve out a unique and compelling sense of place.

Nonsense of Place

The truth is that we have trouble describing our cities, towns, and neighborhoods to others. Imagine you're attending an out of town cocktail party. As you wait in line at the bar a new face introduces himself and asks where you're from. What do you say? If they've never heard of your city or town, how do you describe it?

Chances are, you use one of the seven most common references to describe your town:

1. **The Past** - "Bethlehem, Pennsylvania used to be the second largest steel producer in the United States." Or, "Carson City, Nevada, is an old silver mining town."

2. **Geography** - "We're located about forty miles north of Milwaukee." Or "We're at the foothills of the Cascades."

3. **Natural Resources** - "We're a coal town." Or, "We're a logging town."

4. **Novelty** - "We're home to the World's Largest Ball of Twine." Or, "We have the world's largest chair in our town square."

5. **Celebrity** - "Oprah Winfrey has a summer home here." Or "Abraham Lincoln was born there."

6. **Corporate Citizens** - "We're the home of Fed Ex." Or, "Bentonville, Arkansas, is the home of Wal-Mart."

7. **Attractions** - "We're about a half hour south of Disney World." Or, "Do you know where Edwards Air Force Base is? We're 30 miles north of the base."

There's nothing wrong with describing our cities this way. In fact, all of these descriptions conjure up a picture in the mind of the listener. If you tell me you live near the Grand Canyon or the Great Lakes, I picture those places in my mind. If you tell me you're from Memphis, the home of Fed Ex, I see the purple and orange logo. I imagine giant warehouses and a bustling airport.

Sometimes, we use a combination of these references to paint a picture of our city. Bethlehem, Pennsylvania, is an old steel town and the hometown of Just Born Candy, the maker of those Easter marshmallow treats known as Peeps. All of these kinds of connotations are powerful. They do help create a sense of place.

Unfortunately, defining our towns and cities this way is a double-edged sword. Referencing other places, companies, novelties, celebrities or attractions limits the power of your audience's imagination. The feelings or emotions attached to the references you use are indelibly imprinted on the listener's mind. Simple connotations, like "our town is an artist colony near Santa Fe, New Mexico" paint an immediate picture in your mind. More complicated references, like "Greensburg, Kansas, is the Greenest town in the world," force the listener to work through the connotations and invites them to ask questions that paint a deeper and more valuable impression. This generates an impression painted by you, not contrived by their connotations of places they think they already know. (We'll learn more about the amazing story behind Greensburg, Kansas, a little later.)

The right connotations allow you to tell your town's story.

A sense of place is more a mythos than a science. It's a set of assumptions and beliefs about a town. The perception of your town is defined by much more than the geography, the novelties, the attractions or the past. It is all of those things plus the culture, the people, the local accent, the corporations, and even the audience's perception of those things. A sense of place is intangible. It's malleable and fungible. We can stretch the world's perception of our cities and towns by redefining our sense of place.

Stop using external references to describe your town. Force your audience to paint a new picture. Create a blank canvas and stroke-by-stroke use your assets, your business, and your vision for the future to create a unique place in their mind.

You have the power to define how people think about your town. More importantly, you have the power to influence how people tell others about your city. It's our job to use the right connotations and preconceptions to paint a perfect (and consistently communicated) picture of our place.

We must endow our undifferentiated places with value. We must manipulate the imagination of those we want to attract by extending the connotations they apply to our towns. We must create a new sense of place.

Our goal is to create a place where the people, the history, the geography, and the future coalesce to build an emotional relationship between the people we want to attract and the place we live. Instead of relying on logical reasoning, we must tap into something emotional. We must create something unique. We have to create something own-able.

That's what staking your claim is all about. Now you can own a corner of their mind and set a trigger. Your claim is the sticky statement they'll repeat to others. Now, you need to own a piece of their hearts. You must empower them to connect emotionally with the place you live and work. You win hearts by creating a sense of place. Staking your claim is only the gateway to their emotions. But it's the three laws of location-envy that will complete the picture: the law of the origin story, the law of the cornerstone, and the law of the visionary that will help do this. Arguably, the most powerful rule you can apply to your town's claim is The Law of the Origin Story.

CHAPTER FIVE
The Law of The Origin Story

We love a good origin story.

An origin story is the back-story of a person, place or thing. It's the legend behind a comic book character, a corporation, a product or even a sport.

Did you know that NASCAR's origin story begins with bootlegging? During prohibition alcohol smugglers decided to soup-up their cars so they could outrun the police. Occasionally, these bootleggers (infinitely proud of the cars they'd built) would gather together and race their vehicles for bragging rights. One day at a hotel bar after an impromptu race in Daytona Beach, a fan named Bill France decided to create a set of rules, put a promotional plan together, and organize a few races. Today we call it NASCAR.

When it comes to corporate origin stories it would seem that a garage or a dorm room is one of the best places to build a successful business. Hewlett Packard, Apple Computer, Google, Amazon, Disney, Yankee Candle, Harley Davidson, Mattel, Maglite, and Lotus all tell origin stories that start in someone's garage and end with success. Facebook, Dell, and Microsoft are all purported to have started in dorm rooms. Read enough of these origin stories and you might think your business would be more successful if you move into a garage or find yourself a dorm room. (That's location-envy, by the way.)

These kinds of stories are powerful. They're told and re-told. Great origin stories become legends. They become a piece of pop (or even corporate) folklore. And, more importantly, they become part of a place's identity.

Your town and your business need a good origin story. One that ties the place you do business with the success you've become.

Triumphs, Anomalies, & Myths

The vital origin story of your town is the one that supports your claim—not the story of when it was settled, who founded it or the date it was incorporated.

For example, Warsaw, Indiana, was officially incorporated as a town in 1854 (forty-some years before Revra DePuy set up shop downtown) and, while that history is important, it's not crucial to expanding the story of the town's claim. It doesn't help tie your sense of place into the claim you've staked. Instead, you need to dig deep in your history, dive into your folklore, and understand the geographic anomalies that empower you to own your claim.

There are three common types of origin stories that can support successful claims:

1. Triumphs of the past

2. Geographic anomalies

3. Mythical stories tied to the land

The Power of the Past

Have you ever visited a historic landmark and suddenly felt an overwhelming sense of place?

Perhaps you've been lucky enough to stand on the battlefield of Gettysburg. Maybe you've stood on Cemetery Ridge and tried to imagine what it might have been like to see the soldiers of Pickett's Charge marching towards you? Maybe you felt like you were standing on hallowed ground?

Or, maybe you've been to Philadelphia and stood in the middle of Franklin Court (where Ben Franklin's house once stood)? You might have imagined Mr. Franklin's printing press in the corner. Maybe you imagined what Philadelphia was like when Mr. Franklin published his proposal for an experiment to prove that lightning is electricity? Standing there, in modern-day Philly, you might have realized that Ben Franklin stood on this exact spot over 250 years ago. Suddenly you feel something. That is the power of the past.

You've felt it before: an overwhelming sense of place sparked by the history that surrounds you.

Many of the most common (and successful) claims rest their laurels on a triumph of the past. Revra DePuy set the foundation for Warsaw's claim back in 1895 in a hotel at the corner of Center and Indiana streets. The hotel's long gone, but if you're in the orthopedic industry you might be struck by the same sense of place standing on the Hayes Hotel site that others get going to Gettysburg.

New York's claim as the financial capital of the world started on May 17, 1792, when 24 stockbrokers drafted and signed an agreement that outlined how they would buy and sell public stock. The Buttonwood Agreement, as it's referred to today, was written underneath a buttonwood tree outside of 68 Wall Street. And those 24 stockbrokers named themselves the New York Stock & Exchange Board (which in 1863 was re-branded as the New York Stock Exchange.)

Historic origin stories, these triumphs of the past, bring an air of entitlement to a place. No other city in the world can hijack the story of Revra DePuy's success and claim it as their own. Londoners (who see themselves as laying claim to being the financial capital of the world) can't steal the story of the buttonwood agreement and re-tell it with an English twist. These stories are tied specifically to a place.

In the same way that one feels an emotional tie to the battleground at Gettysburg or Ben Franklin's Philadelphia abode, you too can stake your claim on a triumph from the past.

Leveraging your town's history and tying it directly to your claim immediately gives your assertion credibility. But more importantly, it permeates your claim with a sense of place.

Dig deep in your town's history and look for any tie to today's claim in your town's past (no matter how small).

As our journey continues across America, I'll be sure to point out other successful towns who leverage a historic origin story – a triumph of the past – to validate their claim.

Looking back to help define your future is one of the easiest ways to elevate your claim and win the hearts of those who hear it. But it's not the only way. All over America I've found towns that leverage their geography and topography to tie their success to the place they live. These towns use the second type of origin story. They've learned to leverage their town's geographic anomalies.

Geographic Anomalies

Imagine you're standing on the ridge of the Grand Canyon. The sun's slowly setting and the sky's turning pink. Hundreds of feet below you the Colorado River winds its way towards the sea and the walls of the canyon are awash in hues of purple, pink, brown, and green. And then, it hits you: An overwhelming appreciation for the natural beauty of the canyon. You're awestruck. The Grand Canyon is a geographic anomaly that has the power to inspire a wide range of feelings and emotions. Those feelings create a sense of place.

Maybe you've driven the five-and-a-half hours north from San Francisco to Redwood National Park. Maybe you've hiked through the redwoods and Sequoias to see the trees the size of skyscrapers. Many of these trees were saplings when the Ming Dynasty began seven hundred years ago. Some were around before Christ was born. As the sun peaks through the canopy you stop and then it hits you: Suddenly, you feel insignificant, minuscule, tiny. Your day-to-day issues feel trivial. Your entire perspective shifts – even if only for a moment.

The Grand Canyon, the redwoods, Alaskan glaciers, Louisiana swamps, Florida beaches, the Mississippi delta, the Nevada desert – these are all geographic anomalies that invoke a sense of place. They have the power to make you feel something. Even when I list these places you picture them in your mind. They might conjure up a memory and remind you of the way you felt when you encountered them for the first time.

Any piece of local geography that deviates from our everyday image of your town can be leveraged to create a sense of place. (Your anomaly may not be as awe-inspiring as the Grand Canyon or as self-reflective as the Redwood National Forest, but that's okay.) Leveraging the place itself and turning even the most mundane anomalies into unique assets can capture our imagination and create a powerful sense of place.

Remember my conversation with the gentleman from Fargo, North Dakota? The same person who introduced me to Sugar Beets and staked their claim as the "Sugar Beet Capital of the World"? In that short conversation over coffee at a conference I asked him why Fargo, North Dakota was such a great place to grow Sugar Beets? Without skipping a beat (pun intended) he explained to me that it's the fertile land of the Red River Valley.

"And," he quickly added, *"did you know that the Red River is one of the few rivers in North America that flows north instead of south?"*

That is a geographic anomaly. It's an unusual and unique river that somehow (it doesn't even really matter how) makes the Red

River Valley and Fargo one of the best places in the world to grow Sugar Beets.

You probably take your local anomalies for granted. Why? Because you can't envision them creating a powerful sense of place. In fact, it's not necessarily a breath-taking piece of geography itself (such as in the case of the Grand Canyon) that provides the fodder for a powerful origin story, but the visionary few who think of your unique resources as powerful enough to turn mountains into marketing.

A Mountain of Paper

Iron Mountain, Inc. is a $6 billion, S&P 500, record, document, and data storage company. You probably knew that. (I bet you've seen their trucks.) But, Iron Mountain is also a place. It's a place that lays the groundwork for a powerful, and surprisingly untapped origin story.

Follow the Hudson River north from New York City for just over two hours and you'll arrive in Livingston, New York. Meander past the apple orchards on the tree-lined rural, roads and soon you'll find yourself at the giant entrance to the catacombs underneath 'The Mountain'. Welcome, to the Iron Mountain.

Behind the loading dock doors lies a giant storage facility packed with photocopies, personal letters, tax returns, contracts, legal briefs, photos, film, and much, much, more. But Iron Mountain wasn't always a storage facility.

Iron Mountain actually got its start as an iron ore mine (as early as the 1700s). By the mid-1930's, the iron had been depleted and the property stood idle. That's when Herman Knaust decided to purchase the property – not to store stuff – but to grow mushrooms. It turns out a cold, dark mine is a perfect place for a mushroom crop to flourish and Knaust made a fortune. It's rumored that until the 1950's Herman's mushroom enterprise was the largest in the world!

By 1951, the mushroom market had taken a turn for the worse and Herman decided to find a new use for his, now empty, former iron mine. The cold war was in full affect, and Herman saw an opportunity. With the threat of a nuclear attack eminent (or so it would seem), Herman converted the mine into a massive underground vault designed to protect valuable corporate information from a nuclear attack or in the more likely event of a natural disaster. He named the company "Iron Mountain Atomic Storage Corporation" and Herman opened his first sales office in the Empire State Building.

Herman Knaust turned an old iron mine into the world's first and largest underground storage facility. (That sounds like a claim to me.)

For more than fifty years, truckloads containing everything from corporate trade secrets to priceless works of art have made the two-hour journey from Manhattan to the 95-acre underground bunker known as Iron Mountain.

Herman Knaust took an old defunct iron mine and turned it into an amazing asset, not once, but twice. The result is an amazingly powerful origin story no one but Iron Mountain, Inc. and Livingston, New York, can claim as their own.

While you might know of Iron Mountain, Inc., chances are you've never heard of the town of Livingston. And to be honest,

I'd never heard of the town myself until I started working on this book. It appears that Livingston, New York, has never leveraged their claim as the "document storage capital of the world" or the "storage capital of the America". They never publicized the fact that their town was home to the "world's first and largest underground storage facility". Which might seem like a missed opportunity. There may be a very good reason for that.

Corporations not only decided to store their valuable documents at Iron Mountain during the cold war. Some of them also rented specially designed space as a disaster recovery site – a bomb shelter – for their global enterprises. For 16 years, Exxon Mobil leased a "200,000-square-foot, three-level bomb shelter in the mine. With 65 rooms, a chandeliered dining hall and commercial kitchen, the shelter was designed to accommodate 90 of the company's top executives."[7] Iron Mountain, Inc. was not only selling storage, they were selling a secret location that, if revealed, might become a target to our cold war foes.

But the cold war is over. Livingston, New York, is a small town and the opportunity to turn the Iron Mountain origin story into the fuel for a boomtown is ripe. Secure data storage companies are some of the hottest tech companies in the world (Box.net, Dropbox, EMC). Imagine if Livingston, New York, staked their claim as the "secure data storage capital of the world". Suddenly, the Iron Mountain story is relevant to today's market and a geographic anomaly – the old Iron mine – is once again at the center of their story. It's the emotional tie the town needs to properly stake their claim.

---

7   "The Secrets of Iron Mountain: Internal Vaults Guard Records of Living, Dead." Hartford Courant, February 22, 1999, Lara, Al.

Imagine if companies like Amazon, Google, Bank of America, Dropbox, Salesforce, even the IRS all moved their servers and your most private data to the secure data storage capital of the world. Livingston would boom and the old iron mountain would be teaming.

Take some time to think about what natural assets have fueled your town's growth in the past. It's amazing to think that one town's old iron mine set the groundwork for two separate world claims in less than a century.

For many of our towns tapping a triumph of the past or leveraging a geographic anomaly may seem difficult (it doesn't always come easy). That's okay. Some towns have leveraged mythical stories that create an amazingly powerful sense of place.

The Mythos of the Land

Myths and legends are powerful. American folklore has been passed down from generation to generation. These stories are easy to tell and, more often than not, they're tied to a specific place. They create an emotional connection between the storyteller, the listener, the characters, and the town where it occurs. Our town's mythology can be leveraged to instill a supernatural sense of place. It's your job to hunt down your local legends to back-up your claim.

Maybe you remember hearing Henry Wadsworth Longfellow's *Midnight Ride of Paul Revere* for the first time? You might have pictured the steeple of the Old North Church and the lanterns that signaled Revere to warn the towns of Lexington and Concord. Visit Boston today and you'll be encouraged to walk the Freedom Trail, which will take you right past the Old North Church, across the Charlestown Bridge to the spot where Revere quietly waited that dark night in April 1775. The anxiety might even wash over you, after all, a war was to break out the next morn.

Less than an hour south of Boston you might stop by Plymouth, Massachusetts. You may park in front of the quaint shops by the seaside and wander over to a replica of the Mayflower. Standing next to the surprisingly small ship, you might find yourself welling up with pride and hope for the hearty settlers who braved the unknown to settle a new land. Wander a little farther and there it is, Plymouth Rock. The actual rock our forefathers first stepped on almost 400 years ago. You'll feel it: a sense of place.

It's not just my home state that has leveraged the folklore, legends, and myths of our past to build a booming business. (Many of our most popular folklore sites are tourist attractions.) Betsy Ross' house, Davy Crocket's death at the Alamo, the gunfight at the O.K. Corral, even an infamous prison called Alcatraz have leveraged their colorful legends and the connection we have with the stories we've heard.

In every town I visited, successful or not, I heard stories. I listened to legends about the town's forefathers. I was told about buried treasure and ghosts at hotels. I received invitations to hike to mythical waterfalls and to stay up late listening for the howls of Big Foot.

But one of the most compelling and economically exciting myths I've ever heard is a Native American legend that inspired the Queen of Soul in a small Alabama town.

A Signature Sound

Nestled in northern Alabama is sleepy town with a legendary sound. Muscle Shoals, Alabama, is the Hit Record Capital of the World. Its powerful sense of place lures musicians from all over the world.

Back in 1967, seventeen years after the first recording studio opened in Muscle Shoals, a young singer looking for a hit record arrived at FAME Studios to record a new album. Her name was Aretha Franklin. Aretha had recorded nine other albums that had failed to top the charts and she needed to try something new. In just a few hours in that Tennessee River town studio, Aretha recorded one of the greatest pop songs in music history: "I Never Loved a Man" (the Way I Love You). That song would go on to hit the top of the charts and turn Aretha Franklin into a household name. Muscle Shoals had delivered on their claim as the Hit Record Capital of the World. The Muscle Shoals sound found the Queen of Soul.

Aretha Franklin didn't happen on Muscle Shoals. Her record label sent her there. Why? Because Muscle Shoals had something special. In Muscle Shoals, a rinky-dink, dry town, musicians experienced a 'vibe'. They were entranced by the 'magic' of the place. Six years before Aretha arrived, FAME Studios released their first hit record with "You Better Move On" by Arthur Alexander. It might have been their first hit, but it wasn't their last.

Wilson Pickett, Bob Seger, Charlie Daniels, Percy Sledge, the Rolling Stones, Rod Stewart, Paul Simon, Bob Dylan, Clarence

Carter, Alicia Keys, and Lynyrd Skynyrd are just a few of the artists who found themselves lured to the mythical Muscle Shoals.

In 1951, Rick Hall founded FAME Studios. While Nashville was already the Country Music Capital of the World and Memphis could already lay claim to being the Delta Blues Capital of the World, no one had staked their claim as the rhythm and blues (R&B) capital of the world. Rick Hall decided to fill that void.

Eight other recording studios would pop-up in Muscle Shoals to capitalize on the claim kicked-off by Rick Hall's successful sound. During the 70s the 'Shoals would produce more hit singles than anywhere else in the world. The town was no longer just the R&B capital of the world. They'd earned the right to call themselves the Hit Record Capital of the World. Remember, success breeds success.

What makes the Muscle Shoals Sound impossible to reproduce elsewhere? No one really knows. Some say the backing musicians raised nearby define the sound. (The decidedly soul-sounding backing band, referred to as "The Swampers" is all white, by the way.) Others believe that Muscle Shoals allowed musicians to focus on the music in a way one couldn't in Los Angeles, New York or Detroit. Still others believe every music legend before them has left something special behind. That something turns the frill-free recording studios into a sacred place. Many musicians say a local Native American legend is responsible for the divine inspiration artists find when they arrive.

The Yuchie tribe originally lived on the banks of the Tennessee River. They called it Tennessee Nunnuhsae or The Singing River. As the legend goes, the river is a princess calling for her lover. Sometimes, when the river rages, her song is loud and boisterous.

When the river flows low, she sings softly. But every day you can hear her hum for her lover through a thousand summers.

It doesn't really matter what gives Muscle Shoals its signature sound. In fact, the wilder the theories, the more entrancing the place becomes. What matters is that you can't find the sound anywhere else in the world. The Swamper's mythical sound is inextricably linked to the town. Muscle Shoals has created an amazingly powerful sense of place.

Muscle Shoals' sense of place is so legendary in the music industry that Lynyrd Skynyrd immortalized the town, its sound, and the backing band in their hit: "Sweet Home Alabama".

"Now Muscle Shoals has got the Swampers
And they've been known to pick a song or two
Lord they get me off so much
They pick me up when I'm feeling blue
Now how about you?
Sweet home Alabama
Where the skies are so blue
Sweet Home Alabama
Lord, I'm coming home to you"

- Lynyrd Skynyrd, "Sweet Home Alabama"

Rick Hall staked a claim. His vision carved out a unique sound that was inextricably tied to the place. Rick Hall created the hit record capital of the world. That claim lured musicians from around the world.

Hall never had to explain why they should be recording in Muscle Shoals. The musicians themselves started asking why they're <u>not</u> recording in a little town on the Tennessee River. That is location-envy at work.

You need to create a sense of place.

Make Me Believe

When you create a sense of place you tap into our emotions. You create a feeling, an aura that the place exudes. But let me be clear, there's a big difference between make believe and making me believe.

Slapping marketing slogans, tag lines, and logos on your town's economic development initiatives is make believe. It's a shallow fantasy of what you wished your town to be. Every place has a history and heritage that should inform the way we build our vision of the future. Stop with the make believe and instead make me believe.

Dig deep in the history, heritage, legends, and lore of your town. Find, elevate, and tell the stories that fill your vision with a sense of place. History is a powerful source of pride and the stories you uncover will be told and retold around the world.

Staking your claim is as easy as filling in the blank. Getting others in your neighborhood on board with your vision is not always as simple. To be clear, staking a claim isn't a meaningless marketing slogan such as Oklahoma City's "Friendliest city on earth." It's a gateway to imbuing a sense of pride on your neighbors. A legitimate claim, one with a powerful back-story, will empower your community to embrace your vision. The mythos that surrounds your claim gives validity to the claim itself.

Before Rick Hall released his first hit record, Muscle Shoals could already lay claim to being "The Birthplace of the Blues". W.C. Handy, considered the "Father of the Blues", was born in Florence, Alabama, just an eight-minute drive up the road from Muscle Shoals. Even Sun Records founder Sam Phillips (who first recorded Elvis Presley) lived in the area and gave the mythical Muscle Shoals sound credit for his music success.

When you add the intriguing Native American legend to the story of Muscle Shoals the mythos is set. The claim is valid.

Your claims must have a backstory that unifies the vision of your future with the history or geography of the place. Why should Warsaw, Indiana, be the Orthopedic Capital of the World? Over a century ago, Revra DePuy's fiber splints lay the foundation for an entire industry. And he did it in Warsaw. (Revra DePuy himself claimed to have been the first orthopedic manufacturer in the world.) No other place can own that claim or tell that story.

A claim isn't a shallow tagline or a marketing tactic. It's not meant to be emblazoned on the "Welcome to Town" sign and forgotten. Your claim should become the gateway to the stories that have laid the groundwork for tomorrow.

Myths, legends, and geographic anomalies paint a picture of why you can do what you do best only in your town. You can't just move Rick Hall's FAME Studios to Los Angeles and expect to get the same sounds and see the same kind of success. Why? Because the artists won't be touched by the Native American princess singing in the Tennessee River or feel the same things that inspired W.C. Handy.

Make me believe that there's no better place in the world to record music, build an orthopedic business, store my data, locate an architectural firm, an ad agency, a sock factory, a luxury brand.... That's what creates a compelling claim for your town.

Make me believe.

Staking your claim sets a trigger that's stored in a corner of our mind. The law of the origin story connects us emotionally with the place you do business, but it's the second rule, the law of the cornerstone, that starts tapping into our wallet.

The Tale of Two Towns
The $19K a Year Difference

Drive eighteen miles south from Muscle Shoals, Alabama and you will arrive in the town of Russellville, Alabama. While Muscle Shoals boasts a population of about three thousand more people, the gap between the average household income is far larger. On average, residents of Muscle Shoals make $19,000 a year more than those in Russellville.

For more insight into the Tale of Two Towns research go to www.townincbook.com/taleof2towns.

CHAPTER SIX
The Law of the Cornerstone

To Get Rich Target A Niche

In 1990, a Harvard Business School Professor by the name of Michael E. Porter penned a seminal book about economic development called *The Competitive Advantage of Nations*. In it, Porter describes the globe in terms of clusters: *"geographic concentrations of related companies, organizations, and institutions in a particular field..."* He goes on to explain that *"clusters arise because they raise a company's productivity, which is influenced by local assets and the presence of like firms, institutions, and infrastructure to surround it."*[8]

---

8   Michael E. Porter, Institute for Strategy & Competitiveness, Harvard University, Frameworks & Key Concepts, www.bit.ly/clusterdef

For the next 25 years, economists have expanded on Michael Porter's clustering concept, tying a wide variety of economic success (everything from innovation to capital investment) to this elegantly simple and successful idea.

It turns out that the successful claim you stake is simply the declaration of the cluster you and your town serve better than anyone else in the world.

But, let's think more deeply than clusters. Go beyond them to embrace micro-clusters. Warsaw, Indiana, isn't the Life Sciences Capital of the World. (That's a more traditional cluster.) Nope. It's the Orthopedic Capital of the World™. (That's a micro-cluster.)

Muscle Shoals, Alabama, isn't the music recording capital of the world, or even the pop music capital of the world. (Those would be clusters.) It's the "hit record capital of the world". That's a micro cluster.

The boomtowns I encountered on my cross-country jaunt have all capitalized on a specific micro-cluster. They set a foundation on which to build their success. Every single successful place I visited employed the Law of the Cornerstone.

These towns, and the businesses already there, have hitched their future on a specific micro-industry to fuel their success - they've set a cornerstone for their growth.

The Law of the Cornerstone: If you want to get rich, target a niche.

Before heading to the Greek Yogurt Capital of the World (one of the best examples of micro-clustering I encountered), let's consider why clustering (and micro-clustering) works. We don't have to go far to see clustering in action. All we have to do is go down to your local McDonalds.

The Perfect Intersection

Ray Kroc, the mastermind behind fast food giant McDonalds, is credited with quipping: *"We are in the real estate business, not the hamburger business."* As the single-largest real estate owner in the world, McDonalds Corporation is a property giant. So if you're going to open a fast food restaurant, where's the best place to buy real estate?

Imagine the intersection of two busy streets. Now, let's put a Wendy's, a Burger King, and a Jack in the Box on three of those four corners. The best place to put a McDonalds is that fourth corner. This is the perfect intersection.

For many of us, the idea of adding a fourth fast food chain in a seemingly saturated intersection seems counterintuitive. Why wouldn't you find a competition-free intersection? Why not identify a location that's under-served by the fast food industry and fill the need? For one simple reason: everyone already thinks of our imaginary intersection as a place to get fast food. The other three brands have done all the hard work of luring hungry customers to this intersection. Instead of trying to carve out a new place in the mind of the consumer we can capitalize on the fact that thousands of fast food customers already think of our crossroads as an intersection with options. Sure, the addition of our restaurant might create a temporary drop in individual restaurant revenue, but over long term we'll all win.

This is clustering on a street-by-street basis. Fast food restaurants aren't the only ones who've recognized the value of clustering to build their businesses. Gas stations and convenience stores are clustering connoisseurs. Think about it like this: every gas station is interested in being at a central location that minimizes the travel distance for their target customer. Obviously, this means every gas station owner wants to be in the exact same place. Which means that the best place for a gas station is near all the other gas stations. Hotels do this. Supermarkets cluster. Clothing stores cluster. In fact, a shopping mall is a great example of a small cluster.

Now, think of your town as the perfect intersection in a global economy. What cornerstone can you set? What success stories already exist in your town? How can your business become the cornerstone for a micro-cluster?

Your town is at a crossroads. Take advantage of the same principles that turn busy intersections into thriving fast food destinations. Micro-clustering turns your town into a destination designed for success. It invites others in the same industry to ask themselves why they're <u>not</u> there.

That's exactly what happened in Genesee County, New York, the Greek Yogurt Capital of the World.

The Greek Yogurt King

Hamdi Ulukaya was born into a dairy farming family in Turkey. At the age of 22, Hamdi moved to Albany, New York, for college and after graduation (and at the urging of his father) Hamdi started a feta cheese company in the town of Johnstown,

New York. Upstate New York has long been a dairy farming powerhouse and Hamdi's cheese business was a success. In 2005, Hamdi heard that Kraft was closing a dairy processing plant nearby. Itching to expand, Hamdi bought the factory, hired the remaining employees, and started processing a new kind of Turkish-inspired yogurt. He called it 'Greek yogurt' and branded the new product as Chobani (the Greek word for shepherd). Chobani started shipping to stores in 2007 and by 2013, Hamdi was worth $1.5 billion and his original factory had expanded three times over.

None of this happened in Batavia, New York. But one smart visionary realized that Hamdi had created a cornerstone for a cluster.

A couple hours northwest of Hamdi's Chobani factory is Batavia, New York, in Genesee County. As the Chobani yogurt factory came online, Steve Hyde struggled to turn Batavia's economic decline around. In his role as the president of the Genesee County Economic Development Center the pressure was on. For years, Steve had targeted the food and beverage industry as a good target for growth, but he needed something much more focused and simple to fuel his town's success.

Steve wanted to find a niche to help Batavia get rich. Steve was looking for a cornerstone to fuel his cluster.

Chobani's explosive growth and its rapid market penetration had set off a firestorm of interest in an entirely new category: Greek yogurt. Brands like Yoplait, Dannon, and Quaker wanted in on the action and it was Steve's job to convince some of the biggest brands in the world that there's no better place to manufacture Greek yogurt than Batavia, New York.

So Steve leveraged the Law of the Cornerstone to create a powerful sense of place.

New York State isn't the biggest milk producer in the country. California and Wisconsin have higher milk outputs every year, but New York State has one thing no other place in the world can claim: Chobani.

Steve leveraged a simple story to start convincing wannabe Greek yogurt manufacturers that Chobani's success relied heavily on the fact that the business was built in upstate New York.

Steve's micro cluster story had three key points:

You see, New York dairy farmers have extra milk. If you want to make Greek yogurt you need three times the amount of milk it takes to make regular yogurt. You won't find enough milk in Wisconsin or California, but you will in Batavia.

Yogurt is a perishable product, which means the faster you turn fresh milk into rich and creamy Greek yogurt the faster you can get it onto store shelves. Batavia is in the heart of New York State's dairy farmland and has access to millions of gallons of fresh milk, within a two-hour drive, every single day.

Perhaps the most compelling reason to make Yogurt in Batavia is the town's access to 1/3 of the entire U.S. Population within a ten-hour drive. Remember, your yogurt needs to get on as many shelves as possible as fast as possible. That's an enormous benefit for a town as centrally located as Batavia. Drive nine hours west and you're in Chicago. Six hours east and you're in Boston or New York. In seven hours or less your yogurt can be on shelves in Washington, D.C., Cincinnati, Pittsburgh, Baltimore,

Philadelphia... the list goes on and on. Show me a town in California or Wisconsin with that kind of access?

Steve's implied message: *"If you want to replicate the billion dollar success of Chobani, there's no better town in the world to build a Greek yogurt processing facility."* Steve had everyone in the yogurt business wondering why they would build a yogurt plant anywhere other than Batavia, New York.

Steve's story created a sense of location-envy in the minds of every wannabe yogurt king in the world.

And it worked.

Today, not just Batavia, New York, but Genesee County, is a shining start of a success. Upstate New York is now home to 28 plants owned by Chobani, Fage, Yoplait, Alpina Foods, and Quaker. Even The Muller Group of Germany has decided to open a Greek yogurt plant in Batavia. By 2012, New York State produced more yogurt than any other state in the union. Steve Hyde's vision had become a reality. New York State is a yogurt empire.

Steve Hyde's simple story had attracted the biggest in the business. Even Steve's economic development peers recognized his accomplishments with the state's highest economic development award.

So how do you do what Steve did? How do you lure a multi-billion dollar industry to town? You focus on your existing successes, build out your origin story, and stake your claim on a cornerstone for a cluster.

But be careful. A cornerstone for a cluster can quickly become a one company town.

The One Company Town

Our country is littered with, what used to be, "company" towns. These are towns where the economic prosperity of just one business fed the entire community. In some cases, the Company even provided the city's infrastructure (power, sewage, transportation, and water). Some towns were created from the ground-up by their corporate benefactors to house and serve the needs of the one factory in town (such as Carnegie Steel Company in McDonald, Ohio).

In their heyday, 2500 American towns relied on a single employer for even the most basic necessities. But what happens when the Company picks-up and leaves? What happens when the Company gets acquired or goes bankrupt or when the market for their wares evaporates or the natural resource is tapped? We all know what happens. The population declines, revenues disappear, and our towns age. Before long, we're a shell of what we once were.

Some company towns still flourish. Kohler, Wisconsin, is a shining star of a village. The plumbing giant built a factory in what used to be called Riverside, Wisconsin, in 1900. Today its tree-lined streets brag a five-star golf resort in addition to the picturesque factory.

Other towns, such as Greenwood, Mississippi, struggle with their one company identity. In 2003, Greenwood, Mississippi, lost three factories to Mexico where labor is cheap. Today, Viking

Range Corporation, maker of high-end kitchen appliances, is the only manufacturer left in Greenwood. Viking Range has single-handedly turned the cotton capital of the world into the poster-child for a "Made in America" movement. Unfortunately, Greenwood hasn't staked their claim. They haven't leveraged Viking as the cornerstone for a micro-cluster.

In 1918, Kohler Company built this complex to house immigrant workers for their factory. Today, The American Club is a luxury spa and resort in the picturesque town. Photo Credit: Kohler Co.

If you've got one successful business, in one specific industry already in town, let's say a kitchen appliance manufacturer (like Viking in Greenwood), you should focus on luring other kitchen appliance manufacturers to town. Why? Because the same infrastructure and resources needed to make Viking successful will make Sub Zero, Breville, KitchenAid, and Wolf successful. They all need access to a focused, trained, and skilled labor force. They need a community who understands their needs, their business, and even their products. They need the same support systems, the same access, the same talent to succeed. (We'll learn more about this phenomenon, called the Supply Chain Reaction, in the next section of the book.)

Just a few of the old cotton row buildings in downtown Greenwood, Mississippi that have been transformed into Viking Range Corporation offices. Photo Credit: Joseph A - www.bit.ly/lf7kv9k

Greenwood, Mississippi, is an economically poor town, located in the poorest county, in the poorest state in our nation. Viking Range Corporation is the first stake in their claim to become America's Kitchen Appliance Capital. With an unemployment rate almost two times as high as the national average, imagine the impact a micro-cluster of companies could have on Greenwood's residents.

Company towns can survive. But their stability is tenuous.

Economic development experts have encouraged us to diversify our city's economy. They've fed our fears of the past and told us to avoid relying on even a single industry, let alone highlighting the success of a single company, to rebuild our towns. But they're wrong. This deep-seated desire to build an economically diverse town has fueled our homogeneity. In an effort to attract anyone and everyone, we all look and sound the same.

Remember, homogeneity is the enemy of growth.

Diverse economies are built over time. They're created by growing, getting, and keeping one specific industry at a time (more on this later). Leveraging your existing success stories creates prosperous towns.

Avoid being a one company town. Ask yourself: Whose existing success can power an entire industry? What micro-cluster can we attract?

Let's assume for a minute that you live in Greenwood, Mississippi, but you don't work in the Kitchen Appliance business. Right about now you might be thinking:

"Andrew, why should I spend all this time trying to turn Greenwood, Mississippi, into the Kitchen Appliance Capital of the World? Why don't I just focus on trying to keep my restaurant or my consulting business or my grocery store, afloat?"

"Great question," I'd say. "Because a rising tide lifts all boats." Let's take a look at how a micro-cluster fuels an entire community.

A Rising Tide Lifts All Boats

Staking your claim, telling your origin story, embracing your cornerstone, and encouraging a cluster are all great. But what about the people not directly involved in the cluster you've created? What about the restaurateurs in town or the office supply store nearby? What about the hospital, the hotel, the web designer, and the accountant down the street? How will the cluster benefit them?

Sure, they may be proud to be part of a growing economy. They might even believe whole-heartedly in the approach you're taking to driving growth. But they'll eventually need to be convinced that this is also going to have an impact on their individual business. This is where you need empirical evidence.

That's where organizations like economic development offices and non-profits like OrthoWorx (in Warsaw, Indiana) make a huge difference. These kinds of institutions take the time to understand the exact impact the cluster is having (or could have) on the entire community. Here's what OrthoWorx's research found:

- 25% of the people in the surrounding county work directly in the orthopedic industry.

- Every ten jobs in the orthopedic industry support an additional nine jobs elsewhere in the county. (That's more than 6,100 non orthopedic jobs in a city of 13,000.

- Medical device employees make about $10,000 more than the national average every year, which means more money infused into our community.

All of this adds up to $3.7 billion pumped into the state's economy every year, which puts Indiana second in medical device manufacturing (a giant cluster) nationwide (only to California).

With numbers like that, it's easier to understand how the town's cluster results in revenue, jobs, and a better quality of life for everyone.

Quantifying the impact your niche has on the community at large is more important for the people that live here today than the people you're trying to attract tomorrow. Constantly communicating, reinforcing, and monitoring the important role the niche industry is playing in your town's growth is critical to keeping your current people and businesses. Not just those directly related to the industry your town serves.

Micro-clusters put an end to revenue recycling. Why? Because a rising tide lifts all boats. A carefully staked claim fosters the growth of local businesses that provide goods or services consumed outside of our communities. A simple cornerstone for your cluster attracts a steady stream of new businesses to relocate infusing revenue into our local economy.

When you are famous for providing a specific good or services (better than anyone else in the world) you become the tide.

Embrace the Law of the Cornerstone: Get rich. Target a niche.

The rule of the cornerstone positions your past successes as proof that your claim has merit. It sets in motion the belief that others can only replicate massive success if they do business in your town. When Steve Hyde traveled the nation revealing Chobani's "secret to success" to some of the largest companies in the world he had no idea he would be lauded as a visionary. But that's exactly what happened.

Creating a sense of place isn't just about a smart origin story and a clearly articulated cornerstone for your cluster. It's about the people that power your claim. Steve Hyde is a perfect example of the third law for creating a sense of place: **the law of the visionary.**

CHAPTER SEVEN
The Law of the Visionary

Rick Hall, Revra DePuy, Hamdi Ulukaya, and Steve Hyde are visionaries. In their communities, they're just as important as historic visionaries Henry Ford, Thomas Edison, John Rockefeller, and Ida Rosenthal (who founded Maidenform). People, not products or places, are at the heart of every American town's success story. Don't look to Washington politicians or local elected officials for watered-down, politically correct visions of the future. Instead, tap the visionaries in our midst to create a sense of place. Let's build on the power of their origin stories, the cornerstones they've founded, and the places they've helped create.

Dave Packard and Bill Hewlett wanted to work in the rapidly expanding electronics industry. It was the late 1930s when all the big brand name electronics firms were located on the East Coast. If you wanted to make it in the electronics business you had to ask yourself: "Why am I not on the East Coast?" Dave and Bill were asking themselves that exact question and were about to move east to start their company when a Stanford University Professor stepped in. At the professor's encouragement Bill and Dave decided to stay in Palo Alto and build their first product in Dave's garage in 1939. With a capital investment of $538, Dave and Bill founded Hewlett-Packard and sold their first product to Walt Disney Studios.

Dave and Bill built Silicon Valley in their garage. More startups followed and by the 1950s, successful east coast engineers and venture capitalists started asking themselves why they aren't in the 'Valley?

People are attracted as much to people as to places. In fact, location-envy works only if your dreamers and innovators can envision a model for their success in the people that power it.

In 1937 you could have easily dismissed Dave and Bill's garage enterprise as a novelty with little chance of success. But, the secret is:

- Find these visionaries before they're proven

- Foster their success

- Understand and communicate their vision of our town's future to the rest of the world

We must now embrace the third and final law for creating a sense of place: **The law of the visionary**

Every successful community I encountered could point to one or two specific people in town who embody the three traits that qualify them as the town visionary:

1. Optimism - no matter how downtrodden or seemingly stifled the community might be, the town visionary remains eternally confident and hopeful about the future.

2. Imagination - the visionary has a clear, creative, and robust understanding of the role their business plays in the community which, in turn, drives the concept of what the town could or should become.

3. Tenacity - an unwavering determination to see their vision become a reality.

These aren't the only common traits the visionaries I met share, but they're the most important traits that empower our town's success.

Amazingly, **true American visionaries spend just as much time and energy marketing the place they do business as they do marketing the businesses they run.**

That's exactly what's happened in Hamilton, Missouri. One business, led by an amazingly tenacious woman, has turned around an entire town – one quilt at a time.

Disneyland for Quilters

Hamilton, Missouri, used to be known for two things: their state champion high school football team and James Cash Penney, the founder of department store chain J.C. Penney. In Hamilton, football is big. And the farmhouse in which James Penney grew up is now a museum. But neither of those things has come to define Hamilton, Missouri's success. A new visionary has popped up in town and she's redefining an entire industry while she reinvents the town.

Jenny Doan is the future of Hamilton. She's a visionary and she's attracting global attention. Jenny Doan is the woman behind the Missouri Star Quilt Company and she's the single largest employer in the county. Jenny wasn't born and raised in town. She moved here in the late 1990's when her husband got a job as a machinist at the local newspaper. That's when Jenny took up quilting as a hobby.

By 2008, Mr. Doan saw the writing on the wall. The newspaper's staff had been cut from 25 to just five and the Doan family realized they needed to find a new way to ensure their future. Two of Jenny's grown children took out a loan and bought their parents a quilting machine. Mr. Doan and his sister purchased a former antique shop on the main thoroughfare through town to house the 12-foot long quilting machine. And the Missouri Star Quilting Company was born.

Shortly after they moved into their new storefront, Al, one of the Doan's adult children, noticed that quilting was a hot topic on the Internet. Al suggested that Jenny start videotaping quilting tutorials and posting them on YouTube. (Go ahead and take a look at her YouTube channel: www.bit.ly/MissouriStarChannel) Her online video tutorials were a success even though her quilting technique was anything but orthodox.

Years before, Jenny had decided that traditional quilting was extremely time consuming, sometimes taking months (or even years) to finish a quilt. That's when she started cutting corners (pun intended). Jenny used pre-cut pieces of fabric and new construction techniques to finish a quilt in as little as a day. Jenny's online video tutorials appealed to a new generation of time-starved, instant-gratification-seeking, quilters. (Here's a great example of the kind of videos Jenny creates: www.bit.ly/MissouriStarVideo)It wasn't long before her video tutorials had been watched by millions of people around the globe, some as far away as South Africa and Australia.

With an estimated 21 million quilters in the United States Jenny soon started fielding orders for the exact fabric pieces she'd featured in her online tutorials. The orders never slowed and Missouri Star Quilt Company started cashing in.

Today, Jenny and her team of 124 employees, fulfill 1,000 orders a day. Tourists from around the world flock to town to meet Jenny and learn from the master. Business has boomed and the Doans aren't leaving. They're doubling down.

They've purchased seventeen buildings in the middle of the single traffic light town. On one side of the Missouri Star Quilt Company they've opened a "Sleep and Sew" hotel. On the other side: a restaurant.

What's Jenny's vision for Hamilton?

"What we're trying to do is sort of be the Disneyland for quilting," Doan said. *"Bring them to town, give them a place to stay, some food*

to eat, and you know some things to do where every time they come they have a great experience and love what they see here."[9]

Jenny's vision is bigger than her business; it's a vision the entire town should embrace. Hamilton, Missouri, should stake their claim as the quilting capital of the world.

Jenny is Hamilton, Missouri's visionary. While the J.C. Penney birthplace museum attracts a paltry few visitors each month, Jenny's business has stemmed the tide of revenue recycling. Like any true American visionary, she's optimistic about the town's future. She's embracing a clear and creative vision for the future and she's pursuing it with determination and tenacity.

What is even more amazing, is that the Doan family success in reinvigorating an entire town is happening, not with, but in spite of, the rest of the town's reticence in pursuing Jenny's vision.

We will look at the way a true visionary markets the place they do business just as much (if not more) than they market the business itself. But, first, I want you to do a Google search for Hamilton, Missouri. Go ahead. I'll wait.

The Paradox of Adoption

What do you find when you search for Hamilton, Missouri online? What comes up? The answer: Missouri Star Quilting Company.

---

9   Missouri Star Quilting Company's success helps revitalize downtown Hamilton, Garrett Haake, Jun 12, 2013, KSHB.com

Let's remove the most common search results from the list: Wikipedia, a couple of maps, the city's census data, and the links to the town's school district website. (If you search for any city in the world, you get those search results.) What are you left with? Four of the remaining five links pertain to the Missouri Star Quilt Company. Even the TripAdvisor link includes the number one attraction in town. (Yep, you guessed it. It's Missouri Star Quilt Company.)

The Missouri Star Quilt Company's flagship store in Hamilton, Missouri. Photo Credit: Esther Honig

Jenny Doan and her team are so proud of their town that they've inextricably attached themselves to the place. It's impossible to encounter Missouri Star' without being introduced to Hamilton and vice versa. Even Jenny's Internet advertising campaign invites online audiences to visit "beautiful Hamilton." (Watch the ad. It's wonderfully fun. You won't regret it: www.bit.ly/MissouriStarAd). Hamilton IS Missouri Star Quilting Company. But unfortunately, the town officials haven't embraced Jenny and her vision as much as she's embraced the town. It's a one-way street. Hamilton's done nothing to embrace Jenny Doan's success.

Dig deep enough in those search results and you'll eventually learn that Hamilton Missouri, is in Caldwell County. You'll also find the Caldwell County, Missouri, website. Visit the City of Hamilton webpage and you'll find not one single mention of Jenny Doan or Missouri Star'. You'll find plenty of information about Mr. J.C. Penney and the museum in his honor (In fact, it's the number two attraction, out of two, in town.) You'll find an invitation to visit the Hamilton pool. You'll happen on two town events: an annual gas and steam engine show, packed full with antique farm equipment as well as some sort of Civil War reenactment. But there isn't a single mention of the biggest and most successful business in town. Not one.

On the Caldwell County home page you'll see the same kind of generic mumbo jumbo every city and town spews out to try lure people and industry to their town. "Quality living... character and charm... close enough to the city... abundant water supports manufacturing..." You'll find generic tag lines that mean nothing to anyone: "Welcome to Big Heart Country" and "Building our future by learning from and preserving our past." Online, the perception IS that Caldwell County and Hamilton, Missouri, have no interest in attracting quilting-related business to town - let alone quilting tourists.

Online, perception IS reality.

If Hamilton is going to grow even more, they're going to need to change the perception of the entire town. If they're going to save Hamilton they must embrace their visionary. Jenny Doan's success is central to creating location-envy. She is the poster-child for the quick quilting movement. The only thing standing in the way of even bigger, community-wide, success is the town's acceptance of their claim: Hamilton, Missouri is the Quick Quilting Capital of the World.

Hamilton's reticence to embrace Jenny's vision of what Hamilton could become isn't unusual. (In the case studies section you'll learn more about the failure to commit to a claim.) In fact, until fully realized, a visionary's claim is often seen as odd, offbeat, and a bit eccentric. It's these very traits that make a visionary, their claim, and eventually their business successful. I call this the Paradox of Adoption.

The Paradox of Adoption simply states that at the moment a vision is fully embraced by the world at large it's time to re-imagine the future. Essentially, the more people who embrace Jenny's vision for Hamilton, the less odd it becomes. And that creates location-envy.

Jenny Doan is not the only person entrapped by the paradox of adoption. Some of the most well-respected, and fabled, American visionaries have fought the same battle – but they triumphed – and today we couldn't imagine those places without the attractions they built.

One of those people couldn't even convince his own brother that his vision could be a success, let alone an entire town.

Embrace the Visionaries

Jenny Doan's vision for Hamilton, Missouri, is clear and simple. She wants to create the "Disneyland for Quilters." In my casual conversations with residents of Hamilton, Missouri, I get the sense that they see Jenny's vision as a little eccentric, offbeat, and odd. (And, maybe, you agree.) That is perfectly natural.

Many of our culture's business icons endured the Paradox of Adoption. In 1955, Walt Disney opened Disneyland to much fanfare. Universal Studios, Magic Mountain, Hurricane Harbor, Raging Waters, and Knott's Berry Farm would all follow after the success of Walt Disney's vision. Suddenly, Anaheim, California built a reputation as a destination for family fun. Disneyland had sparked the creation of a cluster. Sixteen years later, Walt Disney would spark the same kind of economic boom in a small Florida town called Orlando.

Before Walt Disney opened Disneyland he couldn't even convince his very own brother (and the business brains of the Disney operation) that Disneyland would be a commercial success. In fact, Roy Disney thought the concept of Disneyland was crazy. **But a sea of skeptics can't stop a true visionary.**

Our job as community leaders, business people, and town residents is to fully embrace our local visionaries. It's our job to encourage their imagination and to help them communicate their vision – no matter how odd the vision may seem.

If Jenny Doan is going to be successful, Hamilton must embrace her vision and work to attract a cluster of quilting-related businesses to town. Hamilton Missouri needs their very own Steve Hyde. They're going to need to work together to lure other businesses to Hamilton.

Here's the rub: Paducah, Kentucky, is already the Quilting Capital of the World.

Paducah beckons visitors as Quilt City, USA. Why? Paducah happens to be the home of The National Quilt Museum, which bills itself as the "world's largest museum devoted to quilt and fiber art". Beyond the museum, there are few quilt-related businesses in town and the American Quilter's Society hosts an annual quilting extravaganza (which pumps $18 million into the economy each year).

If Jenny plays her cards right, Hamilton may one day be the quilting capital of the world, but today she'll have to stake her claim on something else. Something different. Something unique if the town is to lure the competition.

You may remember that Jenny's quilting style is unorthodox. Her frustration with the year-long process of creating a quilt the old fashioned way led her to cut corners (another pun intended). Jenny figured out a way to create wonderful quilts in a fraction of the time. Jenny invented a concept called Quick Quilting. So if Jenny's going to stake her claim and if Hamilton is going to attract other businesses to town, why not become the Quick Quilting Capital of the World? That's unique.

40,000 visitors a year make the trip to see Paducah's quilt museum. Jenny's store in Hamilton lures about 50,000 fans a year. So Jenny's already eclipsing Paducah's tourist trade, but she's going to need the entire community to rally around her vision. Hamilton, Missouri, is going to need to create a sense of place and induce location-envy in the minds of quilting-related business owners around the world.

There are 21 million American quilters, which means there is plenty of room to grow. Less than 1% of American quilters visit

Paducah or Hamilton every year. Don't you think Jenny Doan is onto something?

Let's imagine the kind of companies Hamilton could lure as the Quick Quilting Capital of the World: Quilting software companies like The Electric Quilt Company (Bowling, Green, OH) or Machine Quilters' Business Manager (St. Paul, MN,), quilting kit companies such as Keepsake Quilts (Manchester, NH,), quilt pattern companies including McCall's Quick Quilts (Golden, CO,), online community operators like Modern Quilt Guild or Quilter's Village. There are even book publishers, like Stash Books, who focus on publishing books just for quilters, fabric manufacturers like Michael Miller Fabrics, and companies who manufacture consumer sewing machines like Janome and Singer. Then there's an entire industrial quilting universe with brands like Merrow who makes industrial sewing machines (They still manufacture in Fall River, Massachusetts). This short list only took twelve minutes to put together using nothing but the Internet. And not one of those companies competes directly with Jenny Doan's business. It's a micro-cluster.

There are over 3 million quilting-related businesses on Google. Hamilton simply needs to lure a few hundred of those to their town. Missouri Star Quilt Company is the cornerstone of what could be a quilting empire.

The city of Hamilton itself must embrace and evangelize Jenny's vision for a thriving economy.

Look around your city and dig deep in your history. Ask yourself who's creating their own success in your town? Ask why they're building their business here, rather than anywhere else in the world. Ask yourself, how can our historic successes inform our future? What trends might point the way to a more prosperous outlook? Who's on the front-end of the next big thing?

But more than any other rules for creating a sense of place, you must embrace the Law of the Visionary. Without a vision for the future and an existing success story to fuel your growth your town can't (and won't) attract the dreamers and the innovators.

Who is your town's visionary and what is their vision? How can you help attract the dreamers and the innovators?

What if you aren't the visionary? What if your town doesn't have one? Can you stake a claim, save your town, and realize your businesses potential without a visionary?

The Visionary Vacuum

In the three-years of research I've done trying to uncover the formula for creating a booming economy, I feel confident in telling you that without a visionary it's a slow slog to success.

Our American towns and cities are suffering from a visionary vacuum. We've lulled ourselves into believing that someone else will reinvent our town. Someone else will attract the dreamers and the innovators. It's someone else's job to create opportunity in this city. (After all, we have an office of economic development, don't we?) It's this mentality that has left a gaping hole in our communities. This mindset has created a visionary vacuum.

If you can't find a visionary in your town, you have three options: One, you can move. Two, you can keep looking. Or, three, you can fill the void.

There is a vacancy open in your town. Ironically, the visionary vacuum can be filled by anyone. There are no job requirements. There are no pre-requisites. A little later in this book, you'll meet two ordinary citizens that stepped up to fill the visionary vacuum in a town they don't even live in.

The truth is, if you're reading this book, you're the visionary. Fill the void.

So far, we've focused the bulk of this book discussing how the clever creation of a sense of place can benefit our businesses and affect our town's prosperity. But as I journeyed across America I also noticed that staking your claim has the power to combat pessimism, reinstate a sense of pride, and can unify even the most divided of communities. Even the most novel, and seemingly, trivial claims to fame can transform a community from the inside out.

I first encountered the amazing power of a claim when I met Michael Carmichael in Alexandria, Indiana. It was 2004 and Michael Carmichael was about to get more international press coverage in one week than the Greek Yogurt King, Jenny Doan, Rick Hall, and Revra DePuy combined.

CHAPTER EIGHT
The Power of a Claim

The Irony of Hope

One chilly March morning in 2004, Michael Carmichael of Alexandria, Indiana, fulfilled a three-decade old dream. He finally earned a Guinness World Record. I was standing just a few feet away when he did it and I was thrilled. (I may have even been more excited about this feat than Michael, himself.)

I hadn't actually known Michael for very long, just a few years. But I knew he had no interest in breaking the record just so he could hang a plaque on the wall or brag about it with his buddies. Michael wasn't interested in the novelty and fame that comes with a Guinness World Record.

For Michael, the World Record was one of the last pieces of a puzzle he'd been working on for two decades. He was trying to save his town, and film director, Jim Cosco, and I had been documenting his every move for three years.

Michael grew up in Alexandria and he'd lived there in its heyday. Like thousands of other cities and towns across America, Alexandria had hit hard times. The factories were gone; the jobs went with them; the young kids left for the big city, and anyone who did stay in town now shopped at Wal-Mart or the Dollar store instead of the shops on Main Street.

Alexandria's downtown was a shell of its former self. And Michael realized he might be able to create an attraction so compelling – so big – people would pull off the highway to see it.

If Michael could attract that traffic, these visitors would shop downtown. They would eat at the local restaurants. They might even stay overnight at a hotel. Carmichael truly believed he could be the answer to Alexandria's economic woes.

So what was this amazing attraction with the power to transform Alexandria?

On March 15, 2004, standing in a tiny shed at the back of Mike's house, an arborist slowly extracted a core sample from Michael Carmichael's giant ball of paint. That's right, a ball of <u>paint</u>. The arborist stood in amazement as he held the fragile, multi-colored, three-and-a-half foot long, pencil-width, sample in his hands.

"It's like the inside of a giant Gobstopper," he said.

And with that, Michael Carmichael had proven that the ball of paint was, indeed, real. The ball contained nothing but coat, after coat, after coat, of meticulously applied latex paint. The Guinness Book was satisfied and as of March 15, 2004, Michael Carmichael was the proud father of The World's Largest Ball of Paint.

It had all started thirty-years ago when Michael and his son Michael Jr. Added the first coat of paint to a baseball on a stick. And, they've been painting it ever since. As of 2015, the ball of paint weighs-in at a whopping ton-and-a-half and it's girth is so wide it takes two people, arms linked, to embrace its 10- foot circumference.

So, the attraction that Michael believed could turnaround Alexandria's economic decline used to be a "giant ball of paint." Now, the Guinness Book has officially recognized it as The World's Largest Ball of Paint.

Did Michael's giant ball of paint save the town of Alexandria, Indiana? No. The last time I visited the town it was still struggling. But he tapped into something very special. He resurrected a spirit of identity, belonging, and achievement in his community that hadn't been felt for four decades. He got people talking. And what I witnessed that summer in this little town of 5,000 people was nothing short of amazing.

Michael Carmichael was onto something. His concept of marketing the ball of paint as a way to get people to come to town and spend money is a smart one. Michael Carmichael had staked Alexandria's claim as the home of The World's Largest Ball of Paint. And, while the remaining business owners in town were marketing their own individual businesses, Michael wanted to market the town first – and the businesses there second. Carmichael was leading with vision and a simple, big, idea.

It's taken me ten years to realize that Michael Carmichael's marketing theory wasn't actually a failure. He just hitched his hopes on the wrong kind of claim. His claim was designed specifically to attract a novelty clientele. Unfortunately, it wasn't designed to attract the dreamers and the innovators. Novelty claims don't create a sense of place that drives an economic engine. Novelty claims don't power a micro-cluster. But they can still be valuable.

It turns out that almost any claim, no matter how novel, has the power to change the demeanor of an entire town from the inside out. In fact, even a claim as seemingly trivial as Alexandria's has the power to reinstate three things that have been missing from our American cities and towns for a long time: Optimism about the future, a true sense of community pride, and a productive spirit of unity.

It takes external validation of your town's claim to super-charge the internal transformation of the attitudes around town. Ironically, it takes the attention of the world to reinstate a small town's sense of hope and pride. And that's exactly what happened the week after the arborist left and the Guinness Book acknowledged Alexandria, Indiana as the home of the World's Largest Ball of Paint.

There was one other person in the closet-sized shed behind Michael Carmichael's house the day the arborist took a core sample from the World's Largest Ball of Paint: a reporter from the Alexandria Times-Tribune named Randy Chambers. Little did we know it at the time, but it was Randy who would spark the town's summer of promise.

A Summer of Promise

As the arborist slid the core sample out of the giant 'gobstopper,' the town's beat reporter, Randy Chambers snapped pictures as fast as he could. Randy's typical upbeat article would appear in the next edition of Alexandria's only newspaper, but nothing could have prepared us for the media onslaught that would happen over the course of the next few months.

Randy's front-page picture and accompanying caption in the Alexandria Times-Tribune set off a massive daisy-chain of media coverage. With the release of each story, the size of the media outlets covering Michael's ball of paint got larger and larger. Randy's story led to a story in the Muncie, Indiana newspaper, which led to a story in the Indianapolis newspaper, which sparked a mention in USA Today.

Before long, the BBC, CNN, Good Morning America, The Discovery Channel, CBS Sunday Morning, Japanese radio, Sports Illustrated, Paul Harvey's syndicated radio show, SUN Magazine, even Jimmy Kimmel's late night TV talk show had all covered Carmichael's achievement (just to name a few). Over a hundred million people (quite literally) had suddenly been exposed to Alexandria, Indiana. (If you'd like to see the kind of press the ball of paint garnered take a look at www.ballofpaint. com).

The press wasn't just covering Michael's crowning achievement; they were urging the public to help fulfill his life-long dream. Syndicated newspaper columnist, Dave Barry, even wrote an entire column inviting the world to come visit Alexandria, Indiana. Sure, Dave Barry's a humorist, and the column was written with his tongue firmly planted in his cheek, but he invited the crowds nonetheless:

"So to beat the crowds, be sure to get there early, and allow enough time for your family to truly experience the paint ball. Ten minutes is plenty," Barry wrote.[10]

Did throngs of summer road trippers stop-off in Alexandria as a result of all this media coverage? Maybe a few more than previous summers but the increase was imperceptible. Michael and I naively expected the media coverage to inspire thousands and thousands of people to hit the road for Alexandria. But, that just wasn't the case.

By the end of the summer we all realized that Michael's dream was unrealistic. It was novel, fun, and noble, but unrealistic.

Only in retrospect has it dawned on me that, perhaps, the true impact of the massive media attention wasn't external, but internal. Maybe it wasn't felt around the nation the same way it was perceived by the residents of Alexandria themselves.

One story didn't make much of a difference in the town's people's attitudes or self-worth. (This wasn't the first time the Ball of Paint had garnered national attention.) But the sheer volume of high profile, international coverage, week-in-and-week out, that summer had a noticeable effect on everyone from the Mayor to the town's dentist.

---

10   Dave Barry, Miami Herald, June 4, 2004, A Fuelish Summer Trip, www.miamiherald.com/living/liv-columns-blogs/dave-barry/article1933433. html#storylink=cpy

That summer, Alexandria transformed from a pessimistic, downtrodden, and (quite frankly) angry little town, into an optimistic, proud, global sensation. While people in town were openly skeptical about the hopes hanging on the ball of paint, it <u>was</u> the talk of the town. Each new article, television segment, radio station interview, and magazine photo became a source of delight and amusement.

The town got so wrapped up in all the excitement, that Mayor Steve Skaggs handed Michael the golden key to the city and officially recognized Ball of Paint Day. The band played. Speeches were delivered. Inspired youngsters even put their first coat of paint on their very own baseball.

It turns out we were all hoping the ball of paint would bring salvation to the town in the form of tourism. Instead, it filled the town with joy, rallied the politicians around an optimistic citizen, and, even if only for a short time, gave Alexandria something exciting to talk about.

In Alexandria, the summer of 2004 was the summer of promise.

Novelty claims tend to provide short-lived bursts of media attention that create internal excitement. As the glow from the external validation fades and the story runs its course everyone in town returns to their pessimistic, derisive, shameful state.

The real power of a claim, it turns out, isn't that it immediately attracts the dreamers and the innovators. **The real power of a claim is found in its ability to transform your fellow citizens into optimistic, proud, and productive community members.**

Every town we've visited so far in this book has turned their claim's external validation and media attention into positive, internal, reinforcement. The economic impact of their claims can be seen while the emotional impact on the town's residents can be felt.

No town exemplifies the transformative power of a claim more than Greensburg, Kansas. Against all odds, the residents of this tiny town rallied around a one-page proposal that captivated the nation and boosted their sense of pride. It also convinced a clearly conservative community to embrace a traditionally liberal idea: Greensburg went green.

A Town Blown Away

On May 4, 2007, Greensburg, Kansas, was wiped off the map. A tornado cut a two-mile wide path through town, destroying everything. When dawn broke, a grain silo was the only structure left standing.

The town of Greensburg, Kansas seven days after the tornado destroyed the town.
Photo Credit: Greg Henshall/FEMA

Less than a week later, in a pop-up tent standing in for town hall, Daniel Wallach and Catherine Hart circulated a one-page plan to rebuild Greensburg. This wasn't any ordinary plan. Why rebuild, when they could reinvent their town from the ground up? The Wallach's plan was visionary. Their plan was different.

Daniel and Catherine wanted to put the 'Green' back in Greensburg. Their plan was elegantly simple: Greensburg, Kansas, will be the greenest town in the world.

In addition to the 500 residents gathered in the tent that day were the typical cast of characters that assemble in the wake of any national disaster. Amongst them was Governor Kathleen Sibelius who came to hear how this small town would rise from the massive devastation. Daniel and Catherine nervously presented their vision for the future. They painted a picture of a vibrant, exciting, growing, environmentally sustainable town.

The morning after the town meeting, Governor Sibelius proclaimed that this resilient town would rebuild, but it would also be redefined: Greensburg would become a living lab for the future of green technology. And the Governor said it on national television. The vision had been shared. Their claim had been validated on every national morning news program in America.

That interview sealed the deal. The entire nation had heard the proclamation. Greensburg, Kansas, had put a stake in the ground. They'd set an expectation, not just for themselves, but also in the eyes of the world. Greensburg, Kansas, would build a thriving, sustainable economy.

In the midst of the destruction it would have been easier to focus on just rebuilding. It would have been easier to rebuild the town that existed the day before the tornado. But Greensburg went a step further. That May day, Greensburg decided to stake their claim.

Is Greensburg the greenest town in the world? Yes. Their town has more sustainable buildings per capita than any other place on the planet (And it's getting greener every day). But that's not the point.

Two normal people, Daniel Wallach and Catherine Hart, shared their simple, singular vision for Greensburg. It wasn't a politician or an economic development guru that challenged the town to stake their claim. It was two passionate people. People just like you and me.

Daniel and Catherine are Greensburg's visionaries.

Having voted for Republicans in the last ten presidential elections Greensburg, Kansas, is a Republican town. After the tornado, Greensburg, Kansas, was decidedly still politically conservative. So how do you convince an entire town of conservative Republicans to "go green"?

The "green movement" is a liberal talking point. To most conservatives sustainability initiatives are only pursued by "liberal tree-huggers." So when Daniel and Catherine decided to put the "Green back in Greensburg" they had their work cut out for them. They had to reposition the decades of deeply engrained liberal connotations associated with building 'green' and sway the opinions of an entire town.

So, how did they do it? How did they leverage the expectations of a nation to reinstate a sense of pride? How did they combat pessimism and create optimism in the face of such adversity?

How did they rally their politically conservative base around a liberal talking point?

They did it by building on a piece of town history. By creating a sense of place. They did it by showing the town's residents that they should embrace the ideals of their town's founding fathers. They did it by repositioning one of the town's most notable landmarks.

And they did it by telling a transformative origin story.

Digging Deep in Greensburg

Before the tornado, Greensburg's most famous attraction was the world's deepest hand dug well. Using shovels, picks, and barrels, Greensburg's early settlers dug the 109-foot deep, 32-foot wide water well in 1887. The well provided the town with fresh water for 44 years. In 1937 the well was turned into a tourist attraction. For the next seventy years it attracted an average of 43,000 tourists a year.

The attraction had become a novelty, like so many other American roadside attractions (giant ball of paint included), it was something to do as people drove by on their way to somewhere else, until the museum was swept away by the tornado.

The original museum wasn't much more than a shack, but as the town mulled over the liberal idea of "green washing" the town as some "tree-hugging" community, they realized something opinion-altering: their town's forefathers were this nation's original sustainability engineers.

The world's largest hand dug well represented an entire agricultural movement that their fathers and grandfathers had subscribed to. Their relatives, and the town's founders, were the original 'green' Greensburg residents. They believed in simple tried and true conservative values. They lived within their means. They survived off the land. They preserved what they could and relied on conserving their most precious resources to ensure their future. The world's largest hand dug well represented all these ideas.

It wasn't long before many of the residents began embracing the idea that putting the Green back in Greensburg wasn't an empty marketing slogan. It was a reality deeply rooted in the heritage of the town's forefathers. The 1887 hand dug well that illustrated their commitment to this idea had been sitting on Sycamore Street in the middle of town all along. The world's largest hand dug well became proof that, political affiliations aside, we should honor our forefathers and fulfill their vision for a sustainable Greensburg.

Instead of debating whether to rebuild the museum, the question became how can we build something that showcases the significance of the role the well played in the past while it points the way for the future?

They decided to build a sustainable wonder.

The new museum is an architectural marvel and a showcase of modern sustainable living. Its geothermal energy system, high-performance air conditioning, and even the landscaping make the museum a shining example of green technology, architectural innovation, and it typifies the new vision of Greensburg. The story told inside the museum positions the town's forefathers as the original "sustainable settlers" living off the land. Today, the world's largest hand dug well isn't a sideshow roadside attraction. The historic site is an important part of the claim they've staked.

The Big Well Museum in Greensburg, Kansas. Photo Credit: City of Greensburg, KS

Not everyone in town has been convinced that Greensburg should become a showcase for 'tree huggers'. But one thing everyone can agree on is that the new museum is a genuine green gem. It's a source of community pride. Daniel and Catherine tapped into something deeper (pun intended) than a simple claim. They'd tapped into the mythos of Greensburg.

A community's claim, backed by a powerful origin story, instills an awe-inspiring sense of pride. A sense of pride that was so powerful that it crossed political taboos and unified a conservative town around a traditionally liberal idea.

But remember, **it takes continued external validation to sustain the power of a claim.** It takes national (even international)

attention from the outside world to maintain positive momentum. Greensburg is no exception.

On July 7, 2007, two months to the day since the town's total devastation, one media giant delivered more than a front-page newspaper story or a nightly news feature. They came to town with a media plan and an A-list celebrity that would deliver exactly what the town needed: high expectations.

Green Expectations

Leonardo DiCaprio isn't just a Hollywood movie star who appreciates a good story. He's also an active environmentalist. When Leonardo heard that Greensburg, Kansas, planned to rebuild as the greenest city on earth, he knew it would make a great story.

At the beginning of this book I told you that the difference between prosperity and economic struggle comes down to your ability to create an audacious claim. When you stake your claim, you set in motion a chain of events that sends you and your community on a quest. The journey is arduous, but it's also compelling. In the storytelling business, quests are captivating.

The Wonderful Wizard of Oz, The Lord of the Rings, Raiders of the Lost Ark, Star Wars, The Princess Bride are all magnificent examples of quest stories. It's the journey towards a goal and the challenges we face along the way that make these stories fascinating. Leonardo DiCaprio understood that odds were stacked against the residents of Greensburg, but he also knew that if they were successful, it would make a wonderful narrative.

Only two months after the tornado tore through town, Leonardo's production company inked a deal with the town to tell their story. The debris hadn't been fully cleared yet and success seemed so far away for those that decided to stay in Greensburg, but Leonardo was committed to documenting their success.

The media loves to tell the stories of those who overcome the odds to triumph and everyone from the Mayor to the local business people in Greensburg felt the pressure to deliver. Not just for the residents of Greensburg, but for an entire nation who would be watching their story unfold on national television.

DiCaprio's new television series, called "ECO-Town", would be the flagship program on a new television network from the same people behind the Discovery Channel. The new network was called Planet Green and it would be piped into 50 million American homes.

"The centerpiece of the launch of Planet Green is going to be our effort to help the governor of Kansas and the town of Greensburg, Kan., to rebuild that town green," said Discovery Communications president and CEO, David Zaslav, at the network's press conference on June 13th, 2007. *"It's not just about entertainment; we're going to put our resources into Greensburg and Planet Green and try to make a difference,"* he added.

Over the next three years, DiCaprio and Discovery Communications documented the town's reconstruction. The show, renamed "Greensburg," chronicled the ups and the downs. It showcased the day-to-day struggles facing local business owners, city officials, and lifelong residents as they put the pieces back together.

Leonardo's production company wasn't the only one to continue the coverage of the town's progress. The Science Channel also came to town to shoot a four-part mini-series called "Build It Bigger: Rebuilding Greensburg."

All of this attention maintained the town's focus on the quest at hand. The cameras were on and the world was watching. They had two choices: succeed and show the world what Greensburg could achieve or embarrassing failure.

By 2013, Greensburg became the "world's leading community in LEED-certified buildings per capita."[11] The entire town is powered by 100% renewable energy in the form of wind farms and every streetlight is LED. The journey was complete. But their quest isn't over.

Other tornado-stricken towns have reached out to Greensburg's team for advice and assistance in rebuilding their towns. Cities like Tuscaloosa, Alabama, and Joplin, Missouri, both devastated by tornados in 2011, have used concepts pioneered in Greensburg to rebuild for a more sustainable future.

But Greensburg has something no other town has. They have the honor and the ability to stake their claim as the Greenest City on The Planet. It's a claim they're all too proud to tout after their extraordinary rise from the rubble.

Would Greensburg have been as successful if Leonardo DiCaprio, The Discovery Channel, The Science Channel, and literally thousands of other media outlets hadn't continued to cover their

---

11   USA TODAY Green Living Magazine, April 25, 2013, Patrick Quinn.

quest? If Greensburg hadn't felt the weight of an expectant nation watching their every move would they still have pursued their claim? We'll never know.

Not Another Committee

After the tornado in Greensburg the traditional structures (physical and organizational) lay in disarray. Everything had been simplified. The town focused on the task at hand: rebuilding better than before.

Let's not convene another committee. Too many deliberative assemblies already bog us down with endless evaluations of the economic viability of numerous ideas or plans. Instead, we need people with vision.

Let's not start another initiative or apply for another grant to investigate this new economic trend or that new infrastructure project designed to lure new business to town. There are no silver bullets.

We need people willing to pursue their own vision of the future and we need them to lead the way by actively chasing their success. We need our own homegrown success stories because success breeds success. We need to make our own future.

Decades of decline have taken their toll on many towns. We're tired of hoping. We've been complaining about what's wrong with our towns instead of focusing on what's right. Pessimism is infectious. We must combat pessimism. A sense of pride reinstates our self-worth and boosts our self-esteem. A sense of pride is a source of productive energy. It creates momentum in the right direction.

Pessimism would have been an easy and understandable reaction to the tornado that destroyed Greensburg. Instead, residents swapped optimism for pessimism by staking their claim.

"In optimism there is magic. In pessimism there is nothing." - Abraham-Hicks

Acknowledging and integrating our neighborhood's history and heritage into our claim makes us feel good. The origin stories we attach to our town compliment us. They make us proud of our accomplishments. We're more likely to say 'yes' to something when we're treated with dignity and respect. Associating today's town residents with the people of the past is a powerful way to reinstate a sense of pride.

Staking a claim immediately boosts our sense of self-worth. Tying that claim to our geography, history, and heritage builds our collective self-esteem. An optimistic community is far more likely to be successful than one mired down with a foreboding sense of doom fueled by the problems we face today.

Ironically, the successful town visionaries set their ego aside when they present their visions for the future. It wasn't Daniel and Catherine's idea to make Greensburg green. It was the town's forefathers. Daniel and Catherine reminded the town that they must be proud of their past and in one simple story helped reinvigorate a destroyed town's sense of self-worth. Even Greensburg has something to offer the world.

We must not ignore our communities' issues. Instead, today's challenges must be re-framed within the context of our vision for the future. Our vision for the future must be inseparable from the successes of the past. Otherwise, we've got no claim to stake.

Instead of assuming your city won't embrace your vision, leverage the legends you uncover to reinstate a sense of civic pride.

Validate your claim by embracing the media's desire to tell a compelling story. Go on an audacious quest. One designed specifically to grow your business, save your town, and leave your legacy.

What are you waiting for?

A tornado?

In Humboldt County, California, they're not waiting for anything. They're leveraging their reputation as the Cannabis Capital of America to help re-write America's manifesto for growth.

CHAPTER NINE
The Manifesto For Growth

The Symptoms of a Dying Town

In the 1880s Arcata, California, was a hotbed of activity. More than twenty mills hummed day and night processing massive Redwood trees into the lumber that would build the West. Unfortunately, by the 1960s the logging industry was drying up and the entire county was drying up with it.

You see, 1960s Arcata faced the same three issues that many modern American towns face today. No matter where I went on my journey across America the stories sounded eerily similar: The manufacturing belt became the factory belt; the factory belt became the steel belt; the steel belt became the rust belt.

The remnants of our previous triumphs are clear and present as you drive west from Pennsylvania through West Virginia, Ohio, and Indiana. Vacant buildings, crumbling factories, and boarded-up main streets are the landmarks of yesteryear's booms.

Our dying downtowns are the symptoms of three major problems:

1. Population decline - politicians call it urban decay, depopulation or rural flight, but no matter what it's called, people are leaving our towns and cities for the places where opportunity exists.

2. Declining revenue - As our residents pick-up and move, we lose their business. The revenue that supported our main street businesses and the employees that staffed our local success stories vanish. This loss of revenue fuels a vicious cycle of population decline.

3. Aging populations - The only residents left in town, after our young people flee and our business leaders settle elsewhere, is an aging population of retirees yearning for the vibrant main streets that typified our boom towns half a century ago.

Cadillac of Cannabis

By the late 1970s Arcata was growing again, but this time their claim to fame was illicit. A 1979 New York Times article summed up the entire county's rebirth in a simple headline: *"Marijuana Crops Revived California Town."* This wasn't the reputation anyone left in town wanted attached to their community and they certainly didn't want the increased crime that comes along with the growth and distribution of an illegal drug, but it was happening whether they wanted it or not.

All of this started in the mid 70's when a few pioneering artists who had relocated to Humboldt county figured out how to grow seedless marijuana so potent that city-dwelling hippies would pay big bucks for the prime bud. There was no turning back. Arcata, California, and the entire surrounding county of Humboldt quickly became known as the producers of the "Cadillac of Cannabis."

That was thirty years ago and not much has changed. Humboldt County still grows some of the best marijuana in the world. What <u>has</u> changed is the effect their claim has had on the other businesses in town: businesses like Cypress Grove Chèvre and Los Bagels. What is changing is the town's ability to embrace what makes them unique. What they've done is started to use what they've got to grow the legitimate businesses already based in Humboldt County. **Remember, being known for something is better than being known for nothing.**

Before I explain how a world-renowned cheesery and a Mexican-Jewish deli have embraced the idea that their products come from America's cannabis capital, we need to take a step back and look at the way prosperous towns leverage their claims to build thriving economies.

We need to look at the modern American manifesto for growth.

The Modern Manifesto

This is the modern manifesto for growth. Simple, smart, focused growth.

Economic growth is surprisingly simple. If you want to grow your business, and as a result your town, you have to do three things:

1. Grow 'em

   First, you have to grow the existing businesses in your town. Instead of investing your time and energy in attracting new, non-native businesses to town, we have to focus on making the existing businesses more successful today than they were yesterday. It took more than a decade for Henry Ford to build a successful automobile manufacturing business in Detroit. His eventual success sparked decades of growth for his business and thousands of others.

2. Get 'em

   Next, you have to attract new businesses to town. Instead of de-focused, generic businesses, our towns need to attract more of the same kind of businesses (a micro-cluster). Businesses that are part of the supply chain. Businesses that provide the support for our claim. Ford wasn't the only automotive company to set down their roots in Detroit. GM, Dodge, Chrysler, Cadillac (and many more) followed. And it wasn't just automotive manufacturers themselves. The entire auto supply chain migrated to Detroit and the surrounding area.

3. Keep 'em

   Finally, you have to work to keep the businesses you've attracted. You'll need educational institutions that churn out a motivated (and focused) workforce designed to meet the specific business needs of the industry you've built. It's no surprise that the University of Michigan, Michigan State, and Michigan Tech still produce the most highly sought-after automotive engineers every year. You'll need new infrastructure designed to serve the transportation and technology needs of your growing economy. Your town will need to foster the kind of culture designed to meet the emotional needs of a thriving community.

Let's keep things simple. Let's get back to basics.

Let's learn from the past. Those that dismiss the organic growth of our cities and towns as a bygone era impossible to replicate are wrong. Instead of yearning for the boom days of old, let's learn how to translate our heritage of innovation and prosperity into a simple strategy for the future.

Let's leverage the past to inform our future.

None of the three steps in the Modern Manifesto for Growth is more often overlooked than the very first phase: growing from within. Towns like El Paso have invested millions (maybe billions) of dollars in infrastructure improvements and lifestyle amenities (like a minor league baseball park) to attract big businesses to town. Has it worked? No.

In Humboldt County they're doing it right. Instead of wasting time and energy on attracting any old business to town, a select set of like-minded business owners have banned together to help each other grow. They innately understand that if they want to transform Humboldt County they need to Grow 'Em.

CHAPTER TEN
Grow 'Em

We have already established that in order to successfully stake a claim, you must be able to validate it with a current success story. Warsaw, Indiana, has a thriving community of orthopedic brands. Jenny Doan's family is powering the reinvention of the tiny town of Hamilton thanks to quick quilting. Even Genesee County, New York, has the billion dollar success story of Chobani to tell. But in Humboldt County, no legitimate business person wanted to tie their success to all the negative connotations that come along with the illegal (and controversial) marijuana trade.

If the residents of Humboldt County were going to be successful in growing the legal businesses in town they would need to parlay their infamous claim into a positive, business-friendly story. The townsfolk needed to craft an origin story that would convince other businesses to carry their unique products and even convince more like-minded companies to re-locate to Humboldt County. So a group of enterprising town visionaries got together and formed a non-profit called Humboldt Made. (You can check out their wonderful website at www.humboldtmade.com.)

Humboldt Made's mission is to build and grow the local economy by marketing the place they make their products, just as much as they promote the products themselves. But in order to do this, the Humboldt Made team needed a powerful origin story that turned the embarrassing success of the marijuana trade into an asset everyone could appreciate. So what did they do? They turned to the geographic anomalies that make their county unique.

If you ask anyone in Humboldt County what they're known for, besides the nation's best marijuana, the vast majority will tell you it is the Redwood trees. Native to California, the Redwoods are tall trees. In fact, the tallest tree in the world tops out at 380 feet and is located just thirty minutes north of Arcata in the Redwood National Forest. The Redwoods are majestic and humbling. They're a force of nature and, unlike the illegal marijuana trade, Humboldt's business leaders are very proud of the Redwoods.

Why do the Redwoods grow so tall? According to the National Park's Service, Humboldt's Redwoods need four things to thrive:

1. Large amounts of rain (60-140 inches per year);

2. Summer fog that reduces evaporation;

3. Temperate climate, average temperatures between 45 degrees and 61 degrees Fahrenheit;

4. Rich soil in the river bottom flats;

Humboldt County is the only place in the world where these four natural attributes converge to create a perfect environment for the Redwoods to thrive. Humboldt County is the last remaining refuge of the Redwoods.

The Redwoods are the product of a geographic anomaly. The mountains, the ocean, the rivers all converge to create the right environment for the Redwoods to flourish. The 90 centimeters of rain that drizzle down in Arcata every year fills their six massive rivers with an overabundance of fresh water and deposits the rich soil that the Redwoods need to grow. They're so well-known for dense fog in Eureka, California, that the Navy built an airport in Humboldt County to test defogging systems. (Amazingly, the world's first commercial blind landing took place in 1947 on that very runway in zero visibility fog.) The county's average temperature is 53 degrees Fahrenheit, exactly in the middle of the temperature range required to grow giant Redwood trees.

Ironically, it's these same four attributes that make Humboldt County the perfect place to grow the nation's most valuable cannabis.

So, the very same attributes that allow the Redwoods to proliferate has fueled the unlawful growth of the marijuana trade. As the team of visionaries started to explore this idea further, they quickly realized that these exact traits fueled many of their business' successes.

Now, the Humboldt Made team focused on connecting the dots between the marijuana trade, their beloved Redwoods, and businesses as diverse as a Mexican-Jewish deli called Los Bagels, the Natural Decadence bakery, a dairy named Cypress Grove Chèvre, and even a body lotion manufacturer named Ohana Organics.

Connecting the Dots

Remember, your claim creates a sense of place. But for a claim to grow your business and, as a result, your town, you must connect the claim to the business you do. You must connect the dots between a clear sense of place and the products or services you sell.

Connecting the dots between the place one does business and one's businesses success is how one creates location-envy. Your claim is hollow without a series of businesses to support it. And a hollow claim won't grow your business. A hollow claim most certainly won't save your town.

For Jenny Doan at Missouri Star Quilt Company, connecting the dots between the Quick Quilting Capital of the World and her quilt shop is easy. For the team at Humboldt Made, connecting the marijuana trade to the Redwoods to a business that sells bagels isn't as easy. But it is possible and, when done right, it works.

Los Bagels is a quirky Mexican-Jewish deli on I Street in Arcata, California. On my visit to Arcata, I ate a bagel here every single day. Their bagels aren't just good; they're amazing. But why? What makes a great bagel? How can you tie an amazing bagel to the same things that make the Redwoods thrive? How can you connect a chewy, tender baked good to the marijuana business? First, we need to know what makes a great bagel.

Ask any New Yorker what they think the secret to their bagel-making supremacy is and, nine times out of ten, they'll tell you it's the water. H&H Bagels, who for decades reigned as the supreme specimen of the Manhattan Bagel scene, poached their bagels in New York Municipal Water. Water you can't get anywhere else in the world. (That's location-envy, by the way.) So, apparently, if you want to make the best bagels in the world, you need special water.

Every night at 10 PM, the bakers at Los Bagels start making the 4,500 bagels to be sold the next day. Each bagel is boiled and baked to perfection just before they hit the shelves. Los Bagels makes their bagels in essentially the same way they do in New York.

I'm not the only one who loves the bagels from Arcata. Every month, hundreds of fresh bagels are shipped overnight to New York City. Obviously, these particular Gotham City residents could buy bagels on almost any street corner. So why would they order a dozen fresh bagels from the other side of the country? What's different about Los Bagels?

It's the water.

You see, the same water that makes Humboldt County the Cannabis Capital of the World is the same water that makes amazing bagels. It's the very same water that grows the tallest trees in the world that the team at Los Bagels use in their bakery.

Humboldt County happens to have an abundance of fresh water. Six crystal-clear, powerful rivers run through Humboldt (not to mention a few smaller rivers). It's those rivers that feed the Redwoods. It's those rivers that grow great marijuana. It's not hard to imagine that it's this very same water that makes the bagels so amazingly good.

So now, let's connect the dots:

> "Thanks to the crystal-clear water flowing in Humboldt County's six rivers, we are the Cannabis Capital of America and the home of the towering Redwoods. At Los Bagels, we use the very same water that helps the Redwoods thrive to boil our bagels. It's no wonder New Yorkers order hundreds of bagels from us every month. It's all in the water. We're proud to be Humboldt Made."

Suddenly, the water Los Bagels uses takes on a magical quality. It goes from being a commodity to being the mythical bagel water. Water you won't find anywhere else on earth. There are lots of other Humboldt Made members leveraging a similar water story. There are beer breweries and wineries, beef farmers and distilleries. In fact, the more people that leverage the same asset to market their products and services the more successful you'll be.

Connecting the dots isn't easy, but many of the members of Humboldt Made have worked hard to tie their success to the geographic anomalies that surround them.

Take Cypress Grove Chèvre, for example. This little dairy farm has turned into a global phenomenon making award-winning cheeses like one called "Humboldt Fog." A page on their website explains why their cheese is so good: it's the terroir.

"Terroir is a sense of place..." their website claims. The site goes on to extoll the virtues of Humboldt County. "Humboldt County is a place where the legend of Bigfoot is alive and well..." The company's about us page refers to "the six incredibly clean rivers," and mentions the area's dense fog as "both a friend and a foe".

The terroir outside the offices of Cypress Grove Chevre Creamery in Humboldt County, CA.
Photo Credit: Cypress Grove Chevre Creamery

Together, the members of Humboldt Made are connecting their success to the place they do business. They've embraced the same things that make the cannabis crop so successful. They're leveraging the Redwoods (and even the legend of Big Foot) to create a unique sense of place that adds value to the products they sell.

So how do you connect the Cannabis Capital of the World to the concept of Humboldt Made? Here's my attempt:

"It's the six rivers, the dense fog, and the temperate climate that make Humboldt County the Cannabis Capital of America. It's those same rivers that make the bagels taste great. It's the same fog that helps us craft award-winning cheese. It's that temperate climate that helps the pies at Natural Decadence set perfectly. It's the very same climate that helps the Redwoods thrive. We're proud to be Humboldt Made."

In Humboldt County, they've learned to embrace the same things that grow the best marijuana in America to market the most mainstream products that come out of their town.

Not everyone can tie their success directly to the water, the fog or the terroir, and that's okay. If you're going to band together and foster the success of the other businesses in town, you might consider trying what the Humboldt Made team calls "coopetition".

Coopetition

Every year, a select set of Humboldt Made members pack up their wares and head to Anaheim, California for a massive trade show called Natural Products Expo West (Expo West.) Vendors from every conceivable category pack the show's one million square feet of convention floor space. The 75,000 attendees browse more than 2,700 trade show booths all looking for unique, natural products to sell at their retail stores, restaurants, and markets. It's a massive show.

For a company like Natural Decadence Gluten-Free Bakery, standing out at Expo West isn't easy. That's where coopetition comes in. Visit the Natural Decadence booth at Expo West and they're quick to tell you what makes their delightfully delicious Humboldt Mud Pie so good. It's the craft chocolate from Dick Taylor Craft Chocolates and the coffee from Humboldt Bay Coffee, two other Humboldt Made members. Stop by the Vixen Kitchen booth and they'll tell you that their vegan vanilla gelato tastes great when paired with a slice of Humboldt Mud Pie.

Coopetition is the collaboration between business competitors, in the hope of mutually beneficial results. Micro-clustering breeds coopetition. Remember, a rising tide lifts all ships. Every single one of the Humboldt Made members understands that the more they market the other high-quality products made in Humboldt County, the more successful they will all become. They also know that the more they market the fact that Humboldt County makes some of the best products in the world the larger their economy grows. (If you're interested in learning more about the concept of coopetition, my book Brandscaping: Unleashing the Power of Partnerships might help.)

The team at Humboldt Made doesn't limit their cooperative spirit to cross-promoting their partners and competition at trade shows such as Expo West. Every year, the team organizes a Humboldt County Buyers Tour.

Many of the businesses based in Humboldt are looking to attract interest from retailers like Whole Foods, Trader Joe's, and Wegmans. Instead of individually inviting their contacts at these retailers to come and visit their operation, they team up and create a three-day tour. Buyers, from some of the country's largest companies, tour local kitchens, farms, and workshops to get a close-up look at what goes into Humboldt's finest products. These buyers sample Humboldt's wares, eat at Humboldt's finest establishments, drink Humboldt beer, stay at Humboldt hotels, and meet Humboldt's business leaders.

Does all of this coopetition work? Yes. Scour the shelves at your local Whole Foods and you'll see products from Becks Bakery, Tulip Perfume, Blackberry Bramble, Cypress Grove Chèvre (and many more). Every year, a new success story, sometimes two, come out of Humboldt Made's Buyers Tour. The Buyer's Tour wouldn't exist if the entire team didn't believe in the simple idea that the more we work together to promote each other's business and the place we've built our business, the more successful we all become.

If you're going to grow your business and your city, you must embrace the simple idea of coopetition. Leverage your common asset: the place you do business to drive your micro-cluster's growth. One of the amazing side effects a movement like Humboldt Made has on the local economy is an increase in the amount of press coverage and external attention the county receives. It turns out, that growing your economy from the inside out makes for a great story.

The Power of the Press

Remember, a claim transforms your fellow citizens into optimistic, proud, productive community members. Reinstating a sense of pride is one of the most powerful side effects of staking your claim. As we've already seen, cities like Greensburg, Kansas, and even Alexandria, Indiana, have reaped the benefit of an increase in positive local and national press coverage.

If you're going to grow your business and your economy from within, you can't do it without the media. The right kind of media coverage maintains a healthy level of high expectations for you and your fellow business leaders.

There are a few things the media loves to cover: a disaster, a tragedy, a controversy, a scandal, a mystery, and a success story. There are plenty of sources for most of those stories. It's time you team-up and start preaching your local success stories to the press. It's a simple, surefire way to garner positive attention for you, your business, and your community. Without the right kind of media attention creating location-envy is almost impossible.

You are a success story. If no one hears your story (or the story of your peers), no one's interested in your business or your town.

The story in Humboldt County is no different. One of the greatest contributions the Humboldt Made organization makes to its members is its storytelling assets. Their website is a treasure trove of local successes. The media covers those success stories.

Humboldt County is still the Cannabis Capital of America, but the number of news articles about marijuana is half the number of articles about food-related businesses.[12] Headlines like "Marijuana Crops Revived California Town", have been drowned out by headlines like, "Humboldt Made is finding itself

---

12   Google News Search Results, August 2015, Comparing the volume of search results for two compound searches: "arcata" AND "Marijuana" vs. "arcata" and "food" AND "business"

and growing up fast".[13] Or, "Local Mixologist's products launch on Target.com".[14] And, "Pie in the Sky: Foodie Entrepreneurs come out from the Redwood Curtain".[15] For a town desperate to shake their reputation as the Cannabis Capital of America, the business leaders in Humboldt County aren't complaining. They're sharing their successes.

Never before have organizations like ours had the ability to publish our town's success stories on our own platforms. The digital world has empowered everyone to be a publisher and organizations like Humboldt Made leverage their online presence to share their successes on a regular basis. As of August 2015, their team has <u>published more than 315 stories</u> and <u>eight amazingly high-quality videos</u> (They call them films.). These stories don't garner millions of views. They're specifically designed to help the press and the others in town embrace the often overlooked success stories flourishing down the street and around the corner.

In our research, The Tale of Two Towns, we found that towns with a claim receive 2.2 times the number of press mentions than the

---

13   "Making It - Humboldt Made is finding itself and growing up fast." Grant Scott-Goforth, The North Coast Journal, June 18, 2015 www.northcoastjournal.com/humboldt/making-it/Content?oid=2997236

14   "Local mixologist's products launch on Target.com" Juniper Rose, Eureka Times-Standard, February 5, 2015 www.times-standard.com/general-news/20150205/local-mixologists-products-launch-on-targetcom

15   *Pie in the Sky: Foodie entrepreneurs come out from the Redwood curtain* Jennifer Rumiko Cahill, The North Coast Journal, February 13, 2014 www.northcoastjournal.com/humboldt/pie-in-the-sky/Content?oid=2489545

equivalent town without a claim.[16] Humboldt County is anything but average. In fact, Arcata, California received five times (5x) the number of press mentions than Susanville, California, (our equivalent town with a similar size population).[17] Is Humboldt Made alone responsible for that disproportionate amount of press coverage? No. Does it have an impact? Undeniably.

As business leaders and community members, we cannot discount the power of the press. Organizations like Humboldt Made, OrthoWorx (in Warsaw, Indiana) and Greensburg Greentown (in Greensburg, Kansas) are garnering local, national and even international attention for the success stories born in their town. Get the media involved early. Tell your success stories often, to whoever will listen.

Every success story generated by the press helps to create what I call media momentum: positive energy and proof that, when directed at the right external people at the right time, creates action. The team in Humboldt County must harness their media momentum to attract new businesses to town. They must leverage the attention they've garnered to accentuate the emotional impact of the location-envy they are creating. Remember, emotion leads to action while reason leads to conclusions.

Missing opportunities to elevate the media attention they receive is where too many American town visionaries fall short today. In

---

16   In our research we compared 32 towns with claims to 'equivalent' towns to determine the economic impact of a claim. The Value of a Claim Research Report, TownIncBook.com

17   Google News Search Results, August 2015, Comparing volume of search results for Arcata, California and Susanville, California.

the media-saturated, always-on, digital universe you must make the most of every opportunity to target and invite any and every business associated with the micro-cluster you serve.

Prove it & Preach it

To grow the existing businesses in town you must prove that one can be more successful in your city or town than anywhere else in the world (especially in your industry). Each and every one of your local wins (no matter how small or seemingly insignificant) must be disseminated. You must preach it.

Remember, if you want to attract the innovators and the dreamers, you must create location-envy. Location-envy only exists if those you're looking to attract are bombarded by a constant stream of success stories emanating from your city. You must make them believe that there is no better place to build their business than your city.

One person alone cannot bear the burden of marketing the place you do business. Every single one of the business leaders in your community must be encouraged to share the accomplishments of your town at industry events, trade shows, conventions, and cocktail hours.

Industry trade publications, online communities, and social media platforms all play a role in proving that your city or town has a claim worth considering. The more social proof you preach, the more location-envy you and your community will create.

Stimulating the existing businesses in town by connecting your city's claim to whatever business you do, embracing the simple idea of coopetition, harnessing the power of the press, and creating a chorus of business leaders preaching the same message is only the first phase in the modern manifesto for growth. Next, you've got to attract new businesses to town. You have to get 'em.

In the Recreational Vehicle (RV) Capital of the World, they know how to do just that: they get 'em. And, they built their booming economy by embracing a simple secret we can all use to save our towns.

CHAPTER ELEVEN
Get 'Em

The second phase in the modern manifesto for growth mandates that you leverage your local success stories to attract new businesses to town. You've got to Get 'Em. You must leverage the power of your progress to create location-envy in the minds of others. The entire industry (your micro-cluster) must start to believe that they would be more successful if they were doing business with you, in your city, than anywhere else in the world. Before I show you how boomtowns leverage their hometown heroes to attract the dreamers and the innovators, let me introduce you to Wilbur Schult.

Like millions of other Americans, Wilbur Schult made the trip to Chicago in the summer of 1933 to visit the World's Fair. The 115 mile trip from Elkhart, Indiana, to Chicago felt worlds away from the small town where he owned and operated a small clothing store. Schult took in the wonders of the modern innovations on display at the fair, but it was not these marvels that excited Mr. Schult.

On his way to the fairgrounds one day, Wilbur spotted carnival workers being shuttled to and from the event in covered wagon car-trailers. On the long trip back to Elkhart, Wilbur decided that these car-trailers might be perfect for campers, hunters, and fisherman.

Wilbur purchased a few Covered Wagon trailers and started selling them behind his clothing store. A year later, he rented an empty lot and sold more. To keep up with demand, Wilbur became a distributor for Sportsman trailers (built in Michigan) and by 1936 his top salesman and manager Walter Wells suggested that Wilbur manufacture his own brand of camper.

Instead, Wilbur Schult purchased the entire Sportsman trailer company from Milo Miller and renamed it Schult Trailer Company. Immediately, Wilbur and Walter revolutionized the industry. One of their first models included a coal heating stove, a portable water tank, and even a sofa bed.

Within a decade, Schult Trailer Company was the largest maker of mobile homes in the entire country. The company continued to grow and even garnered international attention when King Farouk of Egypt ordered a custom, 50-foot, mobile home from Schult.

The nation was captivated by the romance of traveling the country towing their own recreational vehicle. And the media fueled the boom.

For us, this isn't where the story ends. It's where it begins. What happened in Elkhart next should help guide our efforts to attract other businesses to town.

Up the Supply Chain

If you are going to grow your business, leave your legacy, and save your town, you must focus your attention on attracting the interest from businesses up the supply chain. Think about Detroit's evolution: Ford's success led auto part manufacturers from all over the country (even the world) to set up shop in Detroit. If you are going to get 'em, you must leverage your town's media momentum to bring the entire supply chain (from the raw materials down) to your city.

By the end of 1936 Elkhart was a hotbed of camper manufacturing. According to RV historian Al Hasselbart, Wilbur Schult along with two of the largest camper manufacturers in Elkhart had trouble retaining employees. *"If you were ambitious and driven you'd learn all you could as fast as you could from one of the three largest camper manufacturers in town. Then you'd quit, and start a camper company of your own,"* says Hasselbart. Elkhart rapidly started attracting the dreamers and the innovators. They Grew 'Em.

By 1940, Elkhart's camper cluster had grown from three primary manufacturers to fifty. *"Trailer manufacturers in those days did not have giant warehouses to store all the raw materials they needed to build their trailers,"* explains Al. *"So, everything from lumber to linoleum would be dropped off in the morning and consumed by the evening."* As demand for everything that went into making a trailer rose, suppliers took notice.

Georgia-Pacific raced up from Augusta, Georgia, and built a warehouse on the rail lines in Elkhart to handle the tons of lumber needed every day. Louisiana-Pacific did the same thing. Everyone from Armstrong Tile (who provided linoleum flooring) to Magic Chef (who provided the stoves and appliances) set up shop in Elkhart to ensure they remained part of the rapidly growing supply chain. These companies and many others hired sales staff and delivery personnel. They built warehouses and bought trucks. Elkhart boomed and for the first time, the media dubbed Elkhart the "camper capital of the world."

During WWII, some of the trailer manufacturers secured government contracts to assist in the war effort. Some went out of business. However, after the war ended, Elkhart's camper cluster boomed again.

"During the 1950's and 60's the recreational vehicle market exploded. Elkhart grew from fifty manufacturers to over 300," notes Al. The following few decades of innovation and industry growth consolidated many of the smaller manufacturers.

Today, Elkhart, Indiana, generates $7.2 billion a year manufacturing 80% of the recreational vehicles (RVs) sold and accounts for a quarter of all employment in the city. Sixty-one separate companies manufacture everything from recreational vehicles to mobile homes.[18] Elkhart is the recreational vehicle capital of the world.

"In addition [to the manufacturers], you have transport companies, you have suppliers who bring everything in, from steel and fiberglass

---

18   Slate.com, RV industry keeps Elkhart Rolling, Natalie Burg, May, 8, 2013, www.roadshow.slate.com/rv-industry-keeps-elkhart-in-rolling

and wood and tile. With this middle market RV industry, you probably bring in 300 some additional suppliers into the marketplace," says Bob Parish, VP of National Accounts for GE Capital's RV Group. *"It's a very strong market feeder,"* he adds.[19]

While the RV business has evolved tremendously in the last seventy years, some things are still the same. *"Those early trailer manufacturers in Elkhart pioneered just-in-time manufacturing,"* says historian Al Hasselbart. *"In the 1940's raw materials delivered to a manufacturer's facility in the morning were consumed by the end of the day. That has not changed today."*

Without the early commitments from companies like Georgia-Pacific, Louisiana-Pacific, Magic Chef, and Armstrong Tile to set up shop in Elkhart, Indiana, the entire process of manufacturing an RV might be different. In fact, if Elkhart did not attract the entire supply chain, it might be the Preparation H capital of the world, but that is an entirely different story.

Thirty years ago the media landscape was very different than it is today. There were fewer media outlets that garnered most of your audience's attention and, as a result, every success story published or presented made a bigger, deeper, more lasting impact. In essence, eighty-five years ago (when Wilbur sold his first camper) it was easier to create location-envy than it is today. However, the strategy for inspiring others to bring their business to town remains exactly the same. You must actively leverage your town's media momentum to convince the cluster's entire supply chain that there's no better place in the world to do business.

---

19   www.Slate.com, RV industry keeps Elkhart Rolling, Natalie Burg, May, 8, 2013, www.roadshow.slate.com/rv-industry-keeps-elkhart-in-rolling

You must work up the supply chain.

Creating a strong hold for your cluster in your city demands that you attract more and more of the suppliers that power your industry. The most effective claims are farthest away from the raw materials. This is the Supply Chain Reaction.

The Supply Chain Reaction

Towns who stake their claim on the raw materials that power their local economies litter America's highways.

Elba, New York, also in Genesee County (the Greek Yogurt Capital of the world), lays claim to being the onion capital of the world. Gilroy, California, is the garlic capital of the world. Believe it or not, Rhinebeck, New York, is the anemone capital of the world. Lincoln, Nebraska, is the steak capital of the world. There are catfish capitals and barbecue capitals. There are apple capitals and peanut capitals.

The truth is; you do not have to go too far or look too hard to find a city or town that appears to have already staked their claim. However, looks can be deceiving. Not all claims are created equal.

As we set out to measure the economic impact of a claim on the cities and towns that own them, we discovered something amazing. The closer the claim lay to a "raw material" the lower the impact on the economy (relative to other claims). Alternatively, the farther down the supply chain a claim lies, the larger the economic impact.

So, the longer the supply chain, the bigger the impact.

By now, the reason for this should be clear. The more dimensions your claim encompasses, the greater the opportunity to attract businesses up the supply chain during the Get 'Em phase.

Recall the conversation I relayed at the beginning of this book with a gentleman from Fargo, North Dakota? Fargo is the Sugar Beet Capital of the world (a raw material). The supply chain involved in growing, harvesting, and transporting sugar beets is much shorter than the supply chain for formulating, manufacturing, packaging, marketing, and distributing energy drinks (a large percentage of which use sugar from the sugar beet). Imagine the related businesses, up the supply chain, Fargo could attract if they were the energy drink capital of the world.

Let me be clear, claiming to be the onion capital of the world is a good start. However, if one wants to maximize the impact of a claim on the local economy one must continuously move farther and farther down the supply chain.

What if Elba, New York, leveraged their existing claim as the Onion Capital of the World to become the Onion Soup Capital of the World? What if the Onion Soup Capital of the World soon became the canned soup capital of the world? Each of those seemingly small steps down the supply chain represents untapped potential for the town of Elba.

Your town's potential is directly proportional to the complexity of the supply chain required to power your micro-cluster. The more complex the chain, the bigger the economic potential for your city.

Even with a relatively short supply chain, the Greek yogurt capital of the world has benefited from a series of supply chain side effects.

Supply Chain Side Effects

Between October 2012 and November 2013, Greek yogurt manufacturers in Genesee County, New York, had created 230 new jobs. For a small rural town, this kind of growth constitutes an economic boom. FAGE (pronounced Fa-yeh) and Chobani alone employ 1,400 people in upstate New York. However, looking up the supply chain it is easy to see the positive side effects this type of focused growth generates. Amazingly, every $29,000 invested in yogurt manufacturing creates one new job.[20]

As the yogurt manufacturers flourish, so do the milk producers. *"Our last two years [2012 and 2013], have seen the biggest commitment of capital in our history,"* said Larry Webster, the CEO of Upstate Niagara Cooperative.[21] Larry's milk co-op provides much of the dairy used by Alpina Foods and Muller Quaker. It takes more than milk to make yogurt, however.

O-At-K, a manufacturer of liquid proteins used to make yogurt (and much more) invested $16 million to expand their Genesee County facility. O-At-K (not a yogurt manufacturer) is already

20   The Rise of the Greek Yogurt Industry in Central New York, NADO Research Foundation Report, David Cole

21   Yogurt boom a boon for milk and more, Diana Louise Carter, Democrat & Chronicle, November 4, 2013.

the largest employer in the county, and the latest expansion helped to add 15 new employees to their payroll.

Milk processors, packaging makers, trucking companies, caterers, and cleaners are all growing as a result of the Greek yogurt boom. Not-to-mention the 174 indirect jobs created as a consequence of the county's growth. This includes, "the extra help the grocery store or restaurant has to hire because more people - yogurt plant workers and people working in [up] the supply chain – are eating higher off the hog."[22]

Move even further up the supply chain and you will find that significant infrastructure improvements result from the micro-cluster's growth.

Unemployment rose a few years ago when several tanneries closed in Johnstown, New York, but so did the cost of water. With the industrial decline in the use of water, local residents were left picking up the tab for the massive reduction in capacity. Then, along came Greek yogurt manufacturer FAGE. Suddenly, the high-cost, high-maintenance, water treatment plant transformed from a town liability into a tremendous infrastructure asset. Today, the Gloversville-Johnstown Joint Wastewater Treatment Facility treats the high strength waste generated by FAGE. The result: stabilized water rates for everyone. However, the benefits did not stop there.

In 2009, the very same wastewater treatment facility invested $11 million and gained international attention when they started generating electricity by turning the growing quantities of

---

22   Yogurt boom a boon for milk and more, Diana Louise Carter, Democrat & Chronicle, November 4, 2013.

methane gas into power for FAGE's plant. Visitors from Mexico to Beijing have traveled to the tiny town of Johnstown to see for themselves how FAGE generates up to 91% of their power from wastewater. [23]

The deeper you dive into the entire Greek yogurt supply chain, the more you uncover the ways in which New York State and its residents have benefited from being the Greek yogurt capital of the world.

It is the supply chain side effects that you must begin to quantify if your city is going experience "micro-cluster creep". 'Cluster creep is the sign of a healthy, growing, economy, and it is the one thing that separates sustainable growth from a flash in the pan.

Cluster Creep

As your local economy grows and the local supply chain matures, something amazing happens: cluster creep. Cluster creep is the continuous expansion of a micro cluster into closely related sectors.

It may seem somewhat obvious, however, having an economy built around the entire supply chain for Greek yogurt opens up a series of new business opportunities. With an efficient infrastructure in place for the processing and transportation of milk, upstate New York is the perfect place to make any product that heavily relies on it. Ice cream, cream cheese, hard cheese,

---

23   The Rise of the Greek Yogurt Industry in Central New York, NADO Research Foundation Report, David Cole

butter, and even dried milk manufacturers have started to take notice.

Yancey's Fancy, a cheese maker, just built a new 100,000 square foot manufacturing plant (and already needs more space). First Light Farms & Creamery makes hard artisanal cheeses in nearby Bethany, New York. Perry's Ice Cream employs 312 people year-round at their facility just across the Genesee County line and ships their ice cream as far south as Texas. [24]

All of the Greek yogurt activity over the past decade set the stage for an influx of dreamers and innovators. All of whom require the same (or similar) infrastructure and assets to create their dairy-based businesses.

"It is kind of like a snowball effect," says Steve G. Hyde, president and CEO of the Genesee County Economic Development Center. He is right. The snowball effect reaches far outside of Genesee County. Ken Johnson, the CEO of a refrigerated trucking company called Leonard's Express, is an hour away from Genesee County. However, Ken's business is booming. Along with adding new vehicles to his fleet, he is trying to hire qualified drivers.

"As new businesses come in, it obviously benefits all of us," said Ken. *"We could probably grow more if we could find the qualified drivers,"* he adds.[25]

24   Yogurt boom a boon for milk and more, Diana Louise Carter, Democrat & Chronicle, November 4, 2013.

25   Yogurt boom a boon for milk and more, Diana Louise Carter, Democrat & Chronicle, November 4, 2013.

Cluster creep marks the maturation of a healthy cluster. Unfortunately, it also signals the rise of a new set of issues that we must address in the final phase of our manifesto for growth: the Keep 'Em phase.

You see, Ken Johnson is not the only one having trouble finding qualified employees in upstate New York. Without the right kind of education and training partners, Leonard's Express, and many other successful businesses, might be forced to move their operations. Not because they want to, but because they have to.

If you are going to maintain a consistent pace of growth and success for your company and your city, you must learn how successful cities manage to Keep 'Em.

If it wasn't for the closure of a famous car company in the 1960's, Elkhart, Indiana, might have lost their stronghold on the RV industry. Let's see how one town's loss turned into Elkhart's win.

The Tale of Two Towns
The $1.1 Billion Supply Chain Reaction

Remember, the longer your supply chain the more valuable your claim. In Elkhart, Indiana, we used Merchant Wholesaler sales as a leading indicator of the strength of the recreational vehicle supply chain. Wholesalers in Elkhart provide the RV manufacturers with everything from the steel and struts to the air conditioners and engines that go into each and every RV they build.

Anderson, Indiana (our town equivalent without a claim) generates an average of $1.1 billion less than Elkhart in merchant wholesaler sales. That's an additional $1 billion dollars the supply chain adds to Elkhart's economy every year.

To find out more about merchant wholesaler sales and the Tale of Two Towns research visit www.townincbook.com/taleof2towns.

CHAPTER TWELVE
Keep 'Em

For many American cities or towns, it is all-to-easy to be lulled into complacency by the success and growth of your micro-cluster. There is a certain sense of security and self-satisfaction that comes along with a growing (and seemingly stable) cluster. However, one of the largest threats to your continued prosperity is a lack of qualified personnel to maintain the expansion of your industry.

By October of 2014, the dairy boom helped fuel Genessee County's unemployment rate drop from 10% (in 2010) to 4.6%. A sure sign that the local economy is growing.[26] Paradoxically, it

---

26   U.S. Bureau of Labor Statistics, October 2014, Unemployment Report

is the low rate of unemployment that opens the door for other towns and cities to poach your town's largest employers. In fact, the very same businesses that have built your cluster are suddenly susceptible to being lured out of town by the promise of an endless supply of qualified employees.

As of January, 2015, the unemployment rate in Lubbock, Texas, is 3%, and the city is struggling to grow. *"When the unemployment rate drops under 4 percent it creates more problems than the problems it solves,"* says Lubbock Mayor Glen Robertson. *"A healthy unemployment rate is in the 4 to 5½ percent range. It does make it difficult not only for small businesses and large businesses in Lubbock to find employees, but it hurts the city as well."*

"It hurts us when we're trying to recruit business to Lubbock because one of the first things they look for is the size of your workforce – your willing and ready workforce," Robertson continued. *"When your unemployment rate is hovering around 3 percent they get worried, as they should."*[27] What's fueling Lubbock's low unemployment rate? The massive local oilfield boom.

As you grow 'em and get 'em, you'll suddenly realize you have to Keep 'Em. If you are going to keep the growing businesses you've attracted in town, you must commit to delivering a constant workforce stream. A workforce designed to meet the near-term needs of the companies in town and the innovations on the horizon.

In a moment, we'll see how Genesee County's Economic Development Director, Steve Hyde, is helping maintain the

---

27   "Unemployment rates according to the Workforce Solutions South Plains", Lubbock Avalanche-Journal, February 1, 2015, Denise Marquez]

growth of his local economy with qualified employees. However, before we look at a modern success story, let's take a look at what might have happened in Elkhart, Indiana, if the iconic Studebaker was still around.

Reversal of Fortunes

By the 1960's, Elkhart, Indiana's RV business was humming. The industry had transformed from manufacturing towed trailers in the 1930's to a new breed of campers: the motorhome. By the late 1950's the first self-propelled campers hit the market. And they captured the imaginations of American consumers. However, Elkhart had a problem.

For thirty years, Elkhart had churned out a willing and able workforce with no experience building self-propelled vehicles. In fact, Raymond Frank, the man credited with manufacturing one of the first motorhomes, partnered with Dodge (in Detroit) to convert trucks into Frank Motor Homes. Frank's innovation, along with Elkhart's low unemployment rate, and the rise in demand for automotive experience might have led to Elkhart's downfall as the RV capital of the world. In the 1960's the entire industry might have moved to Detroit if it was not for one nearby town's reversal of fortune.

Elkhart is only a twenty-minute drive east on US Highway 33 from South Bend, Indiana. In the late 19th Century, South Bend was known as the wagon capital of the world. One company, Studebaker, had helped transform South Bend into a thriving community. In the 1850's, Studebaker had manufactured wagons to fuel San Francisco's Gold Rush. The Studebaker Corporation made wagons for the White House and the iconic carriage pulled by Budweiser's Clydesdales. As the world moved from wagons to carriages to cars, Studebaker reinvented itself over and over for 111 years. However, in December of 1963, Studebaker closed its doors. The unemployment rate in South Bend rose overnight to 9% by January of 1964.

Where did that highly-skilled, automotive workforce go? According to RV historian Al Hasselbart, a staggering number of them started commuting to Elkhart, Indiana, to help build the burgeoning motorhome industry. In fact, *"without the closure of the Studebaker factory in South Bend, who knows where the RV capital of the world might be today?"* says Hasselbart. *"We might be buying our motorhomes made in Detroit."*

Elkhart got lucky. Studebaker's closing provided a pool of 7,000 highly-trained employable people who possessed the right skills at the right time. We cannot build our future and leave our legacy to serendipity. We must provide the right kinds of incentives and training to lure the next generation of educated, skilled, and creative workforces to power the next generation of our businesses. Moreover, we must do it before our unemployment rates drop so slow that our success becomes a liability. This is exactly what Steve Hyde is hoping to do in upstate New York.

The Education Imperative

So far, we've focused our energies on only one of the three major problems facing our communities today: declining revenue.

By leveraging an existing business as the cornerstone for a cluster, Batavia, New York is combatting the town's decline in revenue. Hundreds of millions of dollars have been invested in the community to create processing plants. They've employed hundreds of locals to power their plants, at higher than average salaries, pumping new life into Genesee County.

But our population is still declining and the people that stay are rapidly aging out of the workforce. You need a plan to keep our graduating high school students in town. You need to ensure that the businesses we've attracted are provided with a passionate, educated, and excited workforce. If you're going to remain prosperous you need a plan to keep both the people you've got and the businesses you've lured to town.

In Batavia, Steve Hyde's work isn't finished.

Instead of hoping the new corporate citizens in town would be enough to breathe life into the former Rust Belt town, Steve and his team at the economic development office came up with an audacious plan. The centerpiece of his plan is a 250-acre site in Batavia called the Genesee Valley Agri-Business Park. The industrial park is ready with all the infrastructure a food or beverage manufacturer needs: water (it takes a huge amount of water to make Greek yogurt, by the way), railways, sewers, and access to American and Canadian consumers. Not to mention an "abundant supply of milk".

Muller Quaker Dairy and Alpina Food's facility in the Genesee Valley Agri-Business Park. July 2013.
Photo Credit: James Cavanaugh

Muller Quaker Dairy built the world's largest LEED-certified dairy processing plant in Steve's Agri-Business Park as an anchor tenant and Alpina followed. Those two businesses alone need 236 full-time employees. So Steve set out to create an educational system designed to properly train and prepare local, young, and eager talent for the businesses in town.

In 2014, Genesee Community College announced the creation of a new associate's degree program in food processing. With the help of Muller Quaker and Alpina, enrolled students will get hands-on, industry experience. The school is also offering a program for unemployed or under-employed workers called The Food Processing Boot Camp. All of this is designed to provide an educated and skilled local workforce for the region's growing industry. None of this would have happened without Steve's focused vision for the future.

In Warsaw, Indiana, OrthoWorx is spearheading similar initiatives. As of July, 2014, the OrthoWorx team has partnered with nine educational institutions connecting the technology and talent needs of Warsaw's booming cluster with a new generation of employees. They also hold workshops for middle and high school administrators, guidance counselors, and teachers to help transform the educator's perception of the modern manufacturing career path. Since 2009, 300 students a year participate in local internships and co-ops to ensure their strong hold as the Orthopedic Capital of the World.

Back in New York, Steve's team has restored a sense of pride in Batavia. The town is reinvigorated. The county is growing once again. They're known for something and the energy is infectious. Even elementary school students have embraced the state's new found success as the Greek Yogurt Capital of the World.

From Elementary School Up

In early 2014, Craig Schroth and his fourth grade class hatched a plan.

The students at Byron-Bergen Elementary School had been studying the history and government of New York State when they realized that legislators had never officially designated a state snack. Illinois has popcorn. Texas has Tortilla chips. But, what about New York?

What better way to learn how our government works than to petition a state senator? So they did. And it worked.

Mr. Schroth's class researched and helped propose state legislation making yogurt the official state snack. The entire class participated in creating a charming YouTube video to make their case and after both the state senate and house passed the bill, State Senator Michael H. Ranzenhofer gave the class all the credit.

"The idea for this legislation started in a Genesee County classroom, not at the State Capitol. A lot of credit goes to Craig Schroth and his fourth-grade class at Byron-Bergen Central School District for all of their hard work, research, and study that went into proposing this bill," said State Senator Michael H. Ranzenhofer in a press release. *"Today's vote to designate yogurt as the State snack is an example of democracy in action."*

The debate surrounding the bill even garnered national attention from late-night television comics such as David Letterman and Jon Stewart. Sure, they mocked the 45-minute state house discussion about what constitutes a snack, but the national exposure only makes Genesee County more proud of the claim they've staked.

But more importantly, the youngest talent in Genesee County was exposed to the industry that fuels their success. Education sets the foundation for a successful economy and without a viable, pliable, proud workforce our cities and towns will not be able to keep up with the demands of our cluster's growth. We must invest in our legacy from elementary school up.

Your entire community must continually be on the lookout for opportunities to keep new businesses in town. Generally, you'll have some time to find, educate, and then place new employees. However, that's not always the case.

A healthy cluster often creates instant opportunity to expand and grow your local economy. You must be on the lookout for an overnight influx called "The Split".

The Split

Ironically, organic industrial clustering often occurs when someone decides to leave a successful company to start their own venture in the same industry and in the same town. At that time, the community needs to lend full support to both the original company and to the brand new business split if they're to keep both businesses in town.

When Henry Ford started building cars he contracted a local machine shop to make parts for his assembly line. That Detroit-based machine shop was owned by John and Horace Dodge. The Dodge brothers would eventually invest in the Ford Motor Company and a decade later created their own car company: Dodge. Detroit's auto empire would owe its exponential growth to dozens of other car companies whose founders, engineers, and employees came out of Ford's original factory.

In 1969, "The Swampers", Rick Hall's legendary backing band, left FAME Studios and opened their own recording operation in Muscle Shoals. Six other studios would put down their roots in town, too. Justin Zimmer's feud with Revra DePuy's widow over the future of the industry led to the founding of the second orthopedic manufacturer in the little town of Warsaw. A split at Zimmer Orthopedics led to the creation of Orthopedic Equipment Corporation (OEC) and a later Zimmer-split begat a company called Biomet. Split after split Warsaw grew.

Detroit, Warsaw, Muscle Shoals all owe their industrial expansion to a monumental split. We don't need to engineer a split at our town's successful companies. They will occur naturally, if they occur at all. We need to ensure that if (or when) a split happens, we encourage the new business to stay. Our city's future depends on cultivating the new business' success. We must offer the original business support. We need to acknowledge their contribution to the creation of a cluster. These businesses will be the cornerstones of our success and instead of taking sides, which only serves to fuel often contentious divisions, our towns must come together.

A split creates a resource vacuum that our community will fill. While some of the human capital for the new venture will be fulfilled by poaching from the existing pool, we need to provide an entirely new workforce for both to succeed. Those new employees will need training, housing, transportation, and support services. That new business will need real estate, phone lines, computers, office supplies. A split can add fuel to the economic fire started by a single visionary in a small town.

If a split happens, you must be ready to respond. But you can't just wait for a split to grow our economy. We have to make our own future by embracing the picture our visionaries paint for our towns and help them understand that, in order to grow, we need more businesses just like theirs to help fulfill their dreams.

If you are going to Keep 'Em, you must actively engage in the creation of an education infrastructure designed to maintain a steady flow of eager, excited, and skilled employees to power your claim. You, and your fellow visionaries, must leverage your collective power to maintain a healthy unemployment rate. One that encourages constant investment in your city.

However, your work is not finished when you've partnered with educational institutions, created co-op and internship opportunities, and fostered pride from grade school up. The modern manifesto for growth is a simple three step process designed to be continually repeated. It's time you help other visionaries in town to Grow 'Em, Get 'Em, and Keep 'Em. If you want to turn your town into a city, you've got to see what Steve Hyde in Genesee County, New York, is up to next.

One Claim is Never Enough

A century ago your entire city's economy could rest on the laurels of one major claim. For 111 years, Studebaker fueled the economy in South Bend, Indiana. First, South Bend staked their claim as the wagon capital of the world, which grew into the carriage capital of the world, which transformed into the automotive capital of the world. (Yes, that is right, at one point, South Bend manufactured more vehicles than Detroit.) However, in today's fluid economy resting your success on one industry, let alone a micro-cluster, poses an enormous risk to your long-term stability.

If you are going to solidify your city's prosperity, you must embrace the idea that one claim is never enough. You must continually encourage, support, and select the next claim to champion. You must take an active role in your next claim's growth. You cannot sit idly by and wait for the next visionary to pick up the ball and run with it.

Never, in the history of our nation, has it been easier to find a new niche to explore. In the online world, you are empowered to stake multiple claims. You can attract the dreamers and the innovators in industry after industry by building an online identity for your city that makes you THE place to do business for more than one micro-cluster. You must get rich by targeting niche after niche. In today's rapidly evolving global economy, one claim is never enough.

While the unemployment rate continues to drop in Genesee County, Steve Hyde is busy building enthusiasm and interest in their next claim.

Alabama, New York, is almost half-way between Rochester and Buffalo. That is just a commute away from two large cities, north of Interstate 90 on the edge of Genesee County. In January of 2015, unemployment rates in Rochester and Buffalo are hovering between 7 and 8%. For the Genesee County Office of Economic Development, this looks like an opportunity to build something new. To target a new niche. To stake a new claim. So that is exactly what Steve Hyde is doing.

It would be easy for Steve Hyde to rest on the laurels of his successes building the Greek Yogurt Capital of the World, but he knows this would be an enormous risk. Steve understands that the bottom of the yogurt market could fall out at any time. He knows that the market for milk in upstate New York is finite and that if they are going to continue to grow they are going to have to leverage the assets they have to start something new.

So what's next for Genesee County?

Finding the Right Claim

Remember, it takes a tremendous amount of fresh water to make yogurt? Remember, Genesee County is within a day's drive of one-third of the American population? Remember, the transportation network, the trucking companies, and the power grid that the yogurt empire has created? Steve Hyde plans to leverage all of that to stake their new claim as the semiconductor capital of the world.

It turns out that many of the assets required to manufacture yogurt are also needed to make semiconductors, the microchips used in everything from televisions to mobile phones. For example, it takes 2,200 gallons of water to make one integrated circuit. The facilities that make these semiconductors use enough electricity to power a small city.[28] What do they have an abundance of access to in Alabama, New York? Water and power.

In addition to the infrastructure needed to manufacture semiconductors efficiently, Rochester, a fifty-minute drive away from Alabama, New York, happens to be home to eleven colleges and universities. Most notably, the Rochester Institute of Technology (RIT), is continually ranked among the world's best engineering schools.[29] It would seem that if they can Get 'Em, they could Keep 'Em.

Now, I want you to think about the Modern Manifesto for Growth: Grow 'Em, Get 'Em, Keep 'Em. I want you to recall the three laws for creating a sense of place: the law of the origin story, the law of the cornerstone, and the law of the visionary. I want you to think about the first thing Alabama, New York needs to do to begin building their story as the semiconductor capital of the world. Do you remember?

---

28   Topical Reports, Energy & Water Efficiency for Semiconductor Manufacturing, 2000

29   The World's Best Engineering Schools, Business Insider, July 9, 2012, Matt Linley

If you've learned anything so far, you should immediately begin to wonder who's already manufacturing semiconductors in Alabama, New York. Remember, if you are going to create location-envy, you must build on your current successes. You cannot manufacture location-envy, you earn it. You should also be wondering what emotional origin story will capture my imagination. What historic success would lead me to believe there's no better place in the world to manufacture semiconductors than Alabama, New York?

So here's where Genesee County's latest claim falls short. As far as I can tell Alabama, New York is not home to any existing semiconductor manufacturers. Not one. Furthermore, there's no indication that a solid origin story exists for one to believe that Alabama should be the semiconductor capital of the world. Unfortunately, even after their success in building the Greek Yogurt Capital of the World, it appears that the team in Genesee County has reverted to the old way of trying to attract businesses to town. They are attempting to Get 'Em before they've Grown 'Em.

By now it should be obvious that I'm a huge fan of Steve Hyde and the entire team at the Genesee County Office of Economic Development. I also have a soft spot for the Greek Yogurt Capital of the World. However, for Steve Hyde to deliver the same kind of success for Alabama, New York, he is going to need to follow the Modern Manifesto for Growth.

Is there hope for Alabama, New York? Of course there is. There's a claim for every city and town in this great nation.

I have never been to Alabama, New York. However, underneath all the talk about building a semiconductor plant in town lies the foundation for a triumphant claim backed by a compelling origin story. A story much better suited to be exploited by a rural farming community looking to reinvent itself for the 21st century.

It turns out that Alabama, New York, is the birthplace of Charles Dinsmoor, one of the fathers of industrial agriculture. In 1886, Dinsmoor filed a patent for the 'Dinsmoor Vehicle', the world's first continuous track vehicle or the tractor as we know it.

Dinsmoor's tractors were not built in Alabama, New York. In fact, Charles Dinsmoor did not even live in town when he filed the patent (he lived in Pennsylvania,) but when it comes to creating location-envy none of that matters. Alabama, New York could legitimately leverage this simple fact to lay claim to being the Farm Equipment Innovation Capital of the World.

Remember, if you are going to Grow 'Em, you must reinstate a sense of pride in the existing community by leveraging an origin story that creates a sense of place. However, you also need an existing success story.

Right down the street (20-minutes away) from Alabama, New York, Oxbo Corporation continues to design, manufacture, and distribute some of the most innovative farm equipment in the world. How innovative is their equipment? In 2012, The American Society of Agricultural and Biological Engineers recognized four of their new machines with innovation awards. [Four Oxbo machines honored for innovation, Tom Rivers, The Daily News, February 27, 2012] Charles Dinsmoor's spirit of innovation is alive and well at Oxbo's headquarters right there in the heart of Genesee County.

Charles Dinsmoor's patent and Oxbo's triumph provide the townspeople of Alabama, New York, with everything they need to stake their claim as the Farm Equipment Innovation Capital of the World.

Could it work? Yes. Will it work? Only the visionaries in Alabama, New York can prove it.

The Modern Manifesto for Growth is designed to help any city or town visionary stake their claim. No matter how small, how desperate, how successful or how prosperous, you can grow your business, save your town and leave your legacy.

No city needs a new vision more than the city of Detroit, and one company is perfectly positioned to help reclaim the Motor City's glory days. They don't manufacture cars. They make watches.

CHAPTER THIRTEEN
Case Study: Saving Detroit

Shit to Shinola

In 2012, when I hit the road to find out why some cities are booming, and others are bust, I knew I would have to write a chapter about the City of Detroit. No other town typifies the desperation of America's reinvention better than the Motor City. In the summer of 2013, Detroit became the largest municipal bankruptcy in the history of the United States. A claim no one wants to stake.

By January of 2015, the unemployment rate in Detroit had fallen to 14.3% from its peak in 2010 of 28.4%. Detroit's downfall and decay is easy to spot. Crumbling buildings and shuttered homes seem a constant reminder of the city's prosperous past and its precipitous demise.

If any town needs to stake an audacious claim to resurrect its economy, it is Detroit. If any city needs a visionary to fill the vacuum, it is Detroit. If someone is going to save Detroit, he or she is going to need to create unfathomable amounts of location-envy. Detroit needs a modern-day Henry Ford and it looks like a college drop-out from Texas just might fit the bill.

In 1984, Tom Kartsotis started importing and retailing inexpensive watches from Hong Kong. Within a decade, Fossil, the name of the watch company he founded, grew into a $3.2 billion lifestyle brand selling everything from watches to handbags and clothing. In 2011, at the Plano, Texas, offices of his private equity firm Bedrock Manufacturing, Tom launched a new venture by reviving an old brand: Shinola.

Shinola shoe polish was standard issue equipment for American soldiers in WWII. As legend has it, a disgruntled GI polished his commander's boots with dog feces. The prank went unnoticed by his superior and the phrase "you don't know shit from Shinola" was born. Shinola shut its doors in the 1960's. Tom decided it was time the brand was resurrected and reinvented. The new Shinola would manufacture luxury watches. However, this time Tom wouldn't import watches from China, he would make them right here in America. Shinola was an American brand with a rich heritage and history. To capitalize on any remaining brand equity the Shinola team had to find the perfect place to build their business.

"We knew we wanted to localize our brand," said Shinola's CEO Heath Carr in an interview. *"When we researched cities known*

for manufacturing, and as the birthplace of modern manufacturing, Detroit was at the top of the list."

So as Detroit's financial crisis hit a crescendo, Shinola set up shop in the former General Motors Argonaut research building, also home to an arts college. In 2013, the first 2500 Shinola watches hit the market, and they sold out in a week at $550 each.[30] Eighteen months later, Shinola grossed $80 million, selling watches to clients as American as President Bill Clinton (a proud owner of twelve watches).[31] In 2015, Shinola plans to sell 250,000 watches and a whole host of other Detroit made luxury-goods.

Shinola's product-line has already expanded from wristwatches to leather bags, bikes, iPhone cases, pocket knives, footballs, even pet supplies. Like Fossil, before it, Shinola is a lifestyle brand. The Detroit team is also venturing into retail with plans to open 16 domestic stores by the end of 2015 (and Europe next year).

Shinola's marketing (and the entire ethos of the brand) is about Detroit. The city's name is on every single one of the products they sell. Shinola markets the place they do business just as much, if not more, than the business they do.

Take a moment to read their "Why Detroit' webpage:

---

30   Time flies when it's Shinola, as 2500 Detriot-made watches sell-out, Crain's, March 19, 2013

31   The luxury-goods company Shinola is capitalizing on Detroit, Karen Heller, The Washington Post, November 17, 2014

"Why open a watch factory in Detroit?

Why not accept that manufacturing is gone from America? Why not let the rust and weeds finish what they started? Why not just embrace the era of disposability? And why didn't we buy a warmer coat before we moved here?

Through three Detroit winters, we've asked ourselves these questions. And worked not to find our answer, but to build it.

Because we don't think American manufacturing ever failed for being too good. Our worst didn't come when we were at our best. It happened when we thought good was good enough.

It's a tall order to return to form, but we're up for it. We're starting with the reinvigoration of a storied American brand, and a storied American city. Because we believe in the beauty of industry. The glory of manufacturing.

We know there's not just history in Detroit, there is a future.

It's why we are here. Making an investment in skill, at scale. Creating a community that will thrive through excellence of craft and pride of work. Where we will reclaim the making of things that are made well. And define American luxury through American quality."

This is exactly the kind of corporate marketing that builds a sense of place. It is the kind of marketing that creates location-envy. It is the kind of powerful storytelling that opens the door to the reinvention of Detroit as the Luxury Goods Manufacturing Capital of America.

It would have been easier for Tom Kartsotis to build Shinola in his backyard. Fossil's headquarters are in Richardson, Texas, where they employ 1,400 people. Instead, the Shinola team chose Detroit. *"This is about quality manufacturing,"* said CEO Heath Carr. *"What we have found is that there's a spirit of greatness and optimism in Detroit. Detroit is our home base, and we look forward to continuing to invest here. Being in a city with such a strong manufacturing legacy doesn't hurt either."*[32]

The Shinola team believes that there is nowhere better in the world to manufacture high-quality luxury goods than Detroit. And they are not the only ones.

There are hundreds of smaller companies creating luxury items in Detroit and selling them around the world. A quick search on Etsy.com, an online marketplace for handmade and vintage items from around the world, nets almost 2,000 Detroit-made results in categories ranging from clothing to accessories, jewelry, and art. Big brands are slowly taking notice, too. Beverage behemoth, Pernod Ricard (owners of brands such as Absolut and Jameson), is also setting up shop in Detroit. Pernod Ricard executives scouted the city to launch their latest vodka distillery.

---

32   Our Story, Shinola.com Website www.shinola.com/our-story/about-shinola

After meeting four local entrepreneurs OUR/Detroit Vodka launched in May of 2014.

Indeed, why manufacture luxury goods in Detroit? Because the mere fact that they're made in Detroit allows a luxury manufacturer to command a higher price. Rumor has it that before Shinola set up shop in Detroit, Tom Kartsotis commissioned a study to ensure the Detroit brand alone added value to the products he planned to produce.

The study asked participants "if they preferred pens made in China, the USA or Detroit at price points of $5, $10, and $15 respectively". The result? Before researchers included a Detroit-specific option, when given a choice between a pen made in China or the USA, participants consistently chose the Chinese pen. As soon as they added the option to buy the $15, Detroit-made pen to the mix, subjects immediately decided they would gladly pay the higher price point[33]. For any luxury good manufacturer the choice should be clear: a product made in Detroit is worth three times as much as one made in China. That should be reason enough to help grow and attract luxury manufacturers to the Luxury Goods Manufacturing Capital of America.

In February 2011, while Shinola was in its infancy, one of Detroit's most fabled brands, Chrysler debuted a prophetic television commercial during the Superbowl. Starring one of Detroit's most controversial modern icons, rapper Eminem, the two-minute ad shows a montage of Detroit's grit. The spot

---

33   Fossil founder digs the D, Daniel Duggan, Crain's Detroit Business, May 27, 2012

puts Detroit, its people, its iconic buildings, even its crumbling infrastructure on the screen for everyone to see.

Here's the script for the voiceover that accompanies the imagery: (I strongly suggest you watch the ad.)

"I got a question for you. What does this city know about luxury, huh? What does a town that's been to hell and back know about the finer things in life?

Well I'll tell ya, more than most.

You see, it's the hottest fires that make the hardest steel. Add hard work and conviction and a know-how that runs generations deep in every last one of us. That's who we are. That's our story.

Now it's probably not the one you been reading in the papers. The one written by folks who've never even been here, and don't know what we're capable of. Because when it comes to luxury it's as much about where it's from as who it's for. Now we're from America. But this isn't New York City. Or the Windy City. Or Sin City. And we're certainly no one's Emerald City."

At that point, Eminem drives up in front of Detroit's historic Fox Theatre in a new Chrysler 200. Inside, he walks on stage where a gospel choir is singing, and then turns to the camera with that serious, almost angry look of his and says, "This is the Motor City. This is what we do." It's followed by Chrysler's new tagline, "Imported from Detroit."[34]

In this one 2-minute spot Chrysler tells a powerful origin story. An origin story that defines the new vision for Detroit: the luxury goods manufacturing capital of America. That ad, referred to as "Imported from Detroit" is one of the five most viral super bowl commercials of all time[35]. The commercial strikes an emotional chord. Like Shinola, Chrysler markets the place they build their products more than the product itself.

Detroit has everything they need to save their city. They have a powerful origin story born over a century ago as a manufacturing powerhouse. They have an existing success story in Shinola. They even have empirical evidence that manufacturing luxury goods in Detroit enables one to sell their products at a higher margin. They have a willing and able workforce, the infrastructure required to house, power, and transport the goods they make. They even have two unbelievable brands marketing the city for them.

If you want to save Detroit, all you have to do is start marketing it as the Luxury Goods Manufacturing Capital of America. All they need to do is stake their claim.

Former Shinola Chief Executive Steve Bock sums up the opportunity for any luxury manufacturer interested in moving

---

34   Eminem's Super Bowl Ad For Chrysler Had CEO Worried, Joann Muller, Forbes, February 7, 2011

35   Top 10 Most Viral Super Bowl Commercials of All Time, CBS News, Janurary 11, 2013

to Detroit. "People keep telling us how much Shinola has done for Detroit, but it's the absolute opposite: It's what Detroit has done for Shinola."

What are you waiting for, Detroit? Stake your claim.

CHAPTER FOURTEEN
Case Study: Saving Manchester

The Third Industrial Revolution

In 1807, Samuel Blodget opened a canal and lock system on the Merrimack River in a little town called Derryfield, New Hampshire. At the time, he envisioned building a great industrial metropolis modeled after the first industrialized city in the world, Manchester, England. By 1810, Blodget had lured some manufacturers to set up shop in town and, at his suggestion, the town's name was changed from Derryfield to Manchester. (Even Samuel realized he could capitalize on the origin story of the English city's success.)

By 1846, Manchester would be home to companies churning out shoes, cigars, rifles, paper, sewing machines, locomotives and fire engines. It was also the home of the largest cotton mill in the world. Manchester was booming! Today, Manchester is proud to have been the first industrialized American city.

Unfortunately, Manchester is a shell of its former self. The manufacturing left long ago. The massive cotton mill complex is an awkward mix of apartments, restaurants, retail, office, art, and vacant space. As an outsider, it appears that the town is struggling to reinvent itself.

Aerial view of Manchester's mills taken from the top of Elm Tower. Photo Credit: Mike Spenard

Meanwhile, there's a new industrial revolution underway. Maybe you've heard of 3D printing? Some call it additive manufacturing, but, no matter what it's called, many claim it will revolutionize the way we manufacture products in the next century.   Essentially, 3D printers allow anyone to use an electronic file to "print" a 3D object. The revolution is well underway with companies like MakerBot, Inventables, Stratasys, EnvisionTec, and even giants like GE experimenting with and investing in the technology.

In fact, nineteen minutes south of Manchester in a little town called Merrimack, New Hampshire, is one of the leading 3D printing companies in the world. Founded in 1993, Solidscape has been growing ever since.

Don't you think Solidscape could become the cornerstone for an entirely new cluster in Manchester? What if Manchester, New Hampshire decided to be the home of the micro-industrial revolution? What if Manchester became the 3D printing capital of the world?

There's no better place in the world to start a new industrial revolution than the place that fueled the first industrial revolution: Manchester.

What if Manchester staked their claim? What if they leveraged their cornerstone for a cluster?

Unfortunately, like too many struggling American cities and towns, Manchester is focused on what they believe they lack. Michael Skelton, President and CEO of the Greater Manchester Chamber of Commerce, points to their transportation woes as the "key to economic growth".

"We are part of the Boston economic ecosystem," Skelton said. *"Ensuring a strong, reliable and efficient connection to that area allows businesses to become more successful, to grow, to strengthen their workforce."*[36] Manchester's hoping that if they just had a better transportation system their economy would grow.

---

36   Long-range planning, funds key to transportation challenges, Rik Stevens, Associated Press, Times Union, June 26, 2015

Instead of focusing on what you don't have, embrace your hometown successes. In my journey across America, I found no silver bullet infrastructure improvements. Towns with no infrastructure, no rail system, no baseball stadium, no mega office park have seen massive success by growing their local successes. Manchester, like Detroit, has everything they need to start growing their economy.

What are you waiting for Manchester? Stake your claim.

CHAPTER FIFTEEN
Case Study: Saving Hamilton

A Proactive Approach

I first drove into Hamilton, Ohio, (not to be confused with Jenny Doan's Hamilton, Missouri) in November of 2013. Danielle Webb, whom I met at a marketing conference earlier that year, invited me to town to host a non-profit workshop. Danielle is a progressive marketer. She is a bundle of optimism and energy. She is smart, assertive, and very involved. Over drinks, after a long day of brainstorming, I shared my vision for Town Inc. with Danielle. Without skipping a beat, Ms. Webb invited me to come back to Hamilton to help find and stake their town's claim.

Hamilton, Ohio Looking North across the Great Miami River. Photo Credit: Robert S. Donovan

Hamilton, Ohio, is a forty-five-minute drive north of Cincinnati. The Great Miami River meanders right through the city center and the remnants of the town's former glory as a manufacturing powerhouse line its banks. In the mid-nineteenth century, Hamilton city residents harnessed the river's energy to power their economy. Those early manufacturers built steam engines and hay cutters, reapers, and threshers. By the beginning of the 1900s, Hamilton's manufacturing base had expanded to include vaults, tools, vegetable cans, paper, cardboard, printing presses, and even car parts, along with hundreds of other products. Hamilton roared.

As the interstate highway system grew in the 1950s, I-75 skirted around Hamilton, effectively cutting it off from the major North/South transportation route. Hamilton's island of manufacturing soon lost steam. Over the next quarter-century, industrial consolidation, restructuring, and off-shoring slowly bled Hamilton's manufacturing sector dry. Hamilton, like most other towns I visited, might have lost their largest employers. They may have seen many of their neighbors move out along with the manufacturing base. However, those that remain haven't lost their desire to see Hamilton thrive, and Danielle Webb is one of Hamilton's many champions.

In January of 2015, I returned to Hamilton, Ohio.

Michael Dingeldein, an architect, and Danielle had rallied two dozen of Hamilton's most active citizens to spend the day staking their claim. Michael spearheads a non-profit in Hamilton called CORE. CORE's "mission is to accelerate Hamilton's urban renaissance through targeted investments in real estate projects in the City's urban core". Around the table sat Hamilton's city manager; representatives from the local banks; the team from the town's economic development office; a team from a local marketing and advertising agency; even the city's Mayor (Pat Moeller) joined in on the workshop for a few hours.

Over the course of eight hours, we worked through the process of staking Hamilton's claim. We talked about the things for which Hamilton is already "known": great tasting water and recent hydroelectric innovations powered by the Great Miami River. We discussed the negative connotations the town's working to overcome. (At one point, Hamilton was a hotbed of Mafia activity earning it the nickname "Little Chicago"). We discussed the largest businesses finding their success in Hamilton today. We worked through possible origin stories, we even talked about Hamilton's first claim: the Safe Capital of the World. We struggled to uncover an origin story. We stretched to connect the dots. We labored to create a claim that had the power to generate location-envy.

Late in the day, exhausted and overwhelmed, we decided to look at a recent Proctor & Gamble (P&G) investment. Imflux is a P&G subsidiary headquartered in a 317,000 square foot facility right in Hamilton, Ohio. In 2013, Imflux moved into a vacant industrial building on the outskirts of town and immediately announced an investment of $50 MM in machinery and equipment over the next three years. What does Imflux do? P&G created the company to develop new plastics processing technologies for injection molding used in the packaging of products such as laundry detergent, dishwashing liquid, shampoo, and cosmetics. At P&G's headquarters in Cincinnati, packaging is big business.

In fact, Imflux's technology could save P&G as much as $150 MM annually, as well as reduce capital expenditures by an additional $50 MM a year, according to chief financial officer Jon Moeller.[37] Imflux is on the forefront of consumer packaging innovation. Frankly, exactly what Imflux does is still shrouded in mystery. Nevertheless, the company has filed over thirty patents (and had seven granted) in under three years.[38]

Finally, an existing success story upon which the team can build. Remember, if you are going to Grow 'Em, you must create a compelling origin story as the foundation for your future

---

[37]   "P&G subsidiary Imflux to spend millions on machinery: EXCLUSIVE," November 11, 2013, Barrett J. Brunsman, Cincinnati Business Courier

[38]   Imflux.com IP & Innovation, www.imflux.com/imflux-advantage/ip-protection

successes. The City of Hamilton must find a way to tie Imflux's current investment in the community to their history or a geographic anomaly (or both).

A search of the United States Patent and Trademark Office's database reveals a treasure trove on patents filed in Hamilton, Ohio. During Hamilton's heyday, its city's residents filed patents at an alarmingly rapid rate. Inventors in Hamilton registered patents and trademarks for everything from steam engine parts to vault wall construction processes. Dig deep enough, and suddenly you will uncover a whole series of patents for consumer packaging.

That soda can you are holding, the box that just arrived from Amazon, even the cereal box you grabbed this morning would not be the same without just a few of the packaging innovations that came out of Hamilton, Ohio, at the turn of the century.

Hamilton's early innovators include John B. Foote, who revolutionized the way everything from paint cans to soda cans would be manufactured using his patented can seaming machine. John O. Parker, who worked at a giant paper company in town, revolutionized the labeling of packages with a paper coating machine. Even more astonishing for the 1900's, is the fact that one of Hamilton's most prolific inventors was a woman named Maria Owens. Among Ms. Owen's patent archive is an incredible pressure valve fruit jar used to transport fresh juice. Suddenly, Hamilton's claim is coming together.

Next, it is time to connect the dots. A deeper dive into today's packaging supply chain reveals an even greater opportunity for the City of Hamilton to stake their claim. A company called KWRiver Hydroelectric specifically chose to build their low-head turbine technology in Hamilton on the Miami River. As a packaging provider, you use a tremendous amount of electricity and KWRiver's technology will generate 100% renewable energy by 2015. Need to transport the products you package? Sure. One of Fortune's 500 fastest growing companies is revolutionizing the transportation of goods right here in Hamilton. ODW Logistics' technology, infrastructure, and service are designed to create a seamless supply chain experience for their customers. Need innovative packaging design? Hamilton has that too. Recognized as a leader in the world of consumer package design, Innovative Labeling Solutions services clients like Pepperidge Farm, Precision Foods, Sunny Delight, even P&G.

As we assembled all the disparate pieces of a great claim, we realized Hamilton, Ohio, is the Packaging Innovation Capital of the World.

There's only one remaining challenge. Hamilton, Ohio, like hundreds of other cities and towns across America, must take the next step and commit to their claim.

Clusters Don't Come From Space

As of the writing of this book in August of 2015, eight months after my visit to Hamilton, the team hasn't yet committed to the claim. But there's still hope.

If the residents of Hamilton, Ohio are going to attract the dreamers and the innovators, they must embrace their claim as the Packaging Innovation Capital of the World. They must preach it. They must share their claim with the media to build momentum. If Hamilton, Ohio is going to help fill the twelve open job requisites on Imflux's website, they must stake their claim.[39]

How do you embrace your claim? How do you preach the message? How do you get the media interested in telling the story? One of the easiest ways might be to set up a web page that connects the dots. (Here's one I created after the workshop to help Hamilton embrace their claim: www.townincbook.com/hamilton-ohio-the-packaging-innovation-capital-of-the-world)

If you're going to become something to someone you must commit. If you're going to attract the dreamers and the innovators, you must commit. Commit to a claim. A town with a claim is vastly more successful than a town without one. What do you have to lose? In today's fast-paced, global economy, it is better to be known for something than to be known for nothing.

In 2012, the governor of New York State, Andrew Cuomo, held the first annual Yogurt Summit in Albany, New York. That's right, a Yogurt Summit. At the event, yogurt manufacturers, dairy farmers, even transportation officials, got together to discuss the future of the yogurt business.

"There's a business advantage to being together, like Silicon Valley," New York Governor Andrew Cuomo said. *"These cluster economies don't just happen. It doesn't come down from space. Maybe they begin randomly, but then they are planned, developed and facilitated."*[40]

---

39   Imflux.com, Open jobs as of August, 2015, www.careers.imflux.com/list.aspx

40   "Cuomo Says Dairy Industry Can Make New York U.S. Yogurt Capital", Bloomberg.com, Freeman Klopott Aug 15, 2012

Andrew Cuomo is right. Clusters don't just happen. They're engineered.

To the uninitiated, clustering might appear serendipitous. A century ago that might have been the case. The realities of inefficient supply chains, an immobile workforce, and an industrial revolution resulted in organic clustering. However, today, in a world where one can work from anywhere, and access to a global supply chain is an 18-hour flight away, prosperous communities are strategically growing their niches.

If your business it going to grow. If your town is going to prosper. If you are going to leave a legacy, the one thing you must do is commit to a claim.

CHAPTER SIXTEEN
Work Your Claim

The Gold Rush

On May 12, 1848, Samuel Brannan stepped out of his newspaper office on Washington Street in San Francisco. He took a deep breath and ran into the hustle and bustle of Portsmouth Square. In his hand he held a little glass bottle filled to the brim with gold.

"Gold! Gold! Gold from the American River," the broad-shouldered, beady-eyed Brennan shouted all the way.

Within days San Franciscan's fled the city for Sutter's Mill (near modern-day Sacramento) where five months earlier James Marshall had found the first few flecks of gold. Workers left their jobs. Crews abandoned their ships in the harbor. Even Sam Brannan's own newspaper staff walked-off the job to find their fortune on the banks of the American River.

And so it began: The Gold Rush.

Within two months, three quarters of San Francisco's male population had left town for the gold fields at Sutter's Creek. Upon hearing the rumors, Oregonians, Hawaiians, Mexicans, and Chileans packed their bags and took to the sea. By the end of the year the territory's population had swollen 100 times (from 1,000 to 100,000).

As news reached the East Coast of America, President Polk confirmed California's abundance of gold in his inaugural address and more American's headed west. The Gold Rush turned into a stampede.

By the spring of 1849, 4000 immigrants arrived in San Francisco every single week. Some from as far away as China. Thirty-thousand settlers even assembled at overland launch points in the American plains ready to make the trek west by wagon train.

San Francisco had become the Gold Capital of the World and by 1850 Samuel Brannan became the first millionaire west of the Mississippi.

Here's the thing: Sam Brannan never panned for a single ounce of gold.

He was a visionary businessman with a newspaper.

When Sam Brannan landed in San Francisco in 1846 (two years before the gold discovery at Sutter's Mill) he immediately began setting up shop. As a trained printer, Brannan launched California's first newspaper and called it The California Star. He built two flour mills, a hotel, and a general store. Now, all he needed was an influx of customers.

So, Sam decided to use his newspaper to attract farmers to the fertile land in the San Joaquin valley. In March of 1848, Sam Brannan published a special edition of The California Star in which he expounded on the "promise and potential" of California. Brannan sent ten men on horseback to distribute the paper to "every section of the Union."[41]

But no one came, and soon it wouldn't matter.

A few weeks after the special edition headed east, Charles Smith, Sam's partner in a general store at Sutter's Mill noticed that his customers were suddenly paying for goods in gold. Smith sent word to Brannan who immediately came up to investigate. It's said that upon seeing the gold, Brannan purchased every pan, pick, and shovel he could find for 20 cents apiece.

Two weeks after Sam Brannan's parade through Portsmouth Square he was selling the same pans, picks, and shovels for $15 each (a 7000% mark-up).

Two years later, $50,000 dollars a day in gold were panned out of the Sacramento valley.

Sam Brannan was a successful businessman. But he didn't just transform San Francisco from a muddy little cove into a bustling

---

41   Gold Rush Capitalists: Greed & Growth in Sacramento, Mark A. Eifler

city. He founded the city of Sacramento and left an astonishing legacy:

"He probably did more for [San Francisco] and for other places than was effected by the combined efforts of scores of better men;" [42]

What's even more amazing, is that Samuel Brennan's vision for California was inconceivably huge. In September of 1847 (six months before he learned of the gold at Sutter's Mill) Sam Brannan documented his vision in a letter to a friend:

"Here will be the great Emporium of the Pacific and eventually of the world." [43]

Sam Brannan was right. If California were its own country, its modern GDP would rank in the top ten globally, just ahead of India.

Sam Brannan instinctively understood the value of marketing the place he does business more than the business itself. That is the true mark of an American visionary.

Are you a modern-day Sam Brennan? Are you a true American visionary?

---

42   Bancroft, H. H. California pioneer register and index, 1542-1848 (Baltimore : Regional Pub. Co., 1964), 68.

43   www.rsc.byu.edu/archived/california-saints-150-year-legacy-golden-state/chapter-6-year-decision

Economic Development

No one is going to save your town and spark explosive growth but you.

And you <u>can</u> do it.

America's greatest cities were built by people. People who had a vision for their business. Their businesses built thriving towns and these towns turned into today's cities. These people, the businesses they championed, and the towns in which they lived turned America into the greatest nation on earth.

Economic development or the concerted effort by communities to promote a healthy standard of living, even sounds overly complicated. Doublespeak like "inclusive growth" are thrown around by politicians but mean little to the people they serve. Industry jargon like "innovation hubs" and "green growth" are the flavor-of-the-year with an army of consultants promising to help spark new investment in our communities. The problem is that next year there will be a new politician with a new plan. Next month, a new consultant will roll into town preaching a hot trend that should take the place of last year's initiative.

Politicians using shallow buzzwords didn't turn New York's Wall Street into the financial capital of the world. It was 24 stockbrokers gathered under a buttonwood tree in 1792 that set Manhattan's financial fortune in motion. Economic development policy wonks showcasing the hot trend of the day didn't decide to turn Detroit into the automotive capital of America. Instead, Henry Ford capitalized on a thriving horse-drawn carriage trade in 1899 when he started the Detroit Automobile Company. Tax incentives didn't drive the 49ers to head west to San Francisco during the gold rush. One man, a newspaper reporter named Samuel Brannan, publicized a small gold find at Sutter's Mill near modern-day Sacramento, and as news of the discovery spread, hundreds of thousands of people decided to move west to seek their fortune.

Dig deep enough in our nation's history and you will find that regular people built our great nation. People just like you and me.

Over a century ago towns were known for something. Lowell, Massachusetts, was a textile mill town. Waltham, Massachusetts, was known for the railway watches built in the factory down by the river. Seattle was a logging town. New Orleans was a cotton town. Even the small island of Nantucket was known as a whaling town. If you wanted to start a textile mill, a watch factory, a saw mill, a cotton plantation or build your whale oil business, you knew exactly where to go. These towns attracted a growing and skilled labor force to fuel their ambition. The companies in town insured that the infrastructure to support their growing business was tailored to their needs. As business boomed, so did the ancillary support services. Retail shops, home builders, doctors, schools, and churches popped up to serve the ever-growing populations. That is economic development. That is growth.

In the old days, economic development was simple. It's time we take the bureaucracy out of our growth plans. No office of economic development championed the Buttonwood Agreement on Wall Street. No workforce development office assisted Henry Ford in the founding of his auto empire. No sustainable neighborhood commission or town council voted on whether

San Francisco should publicize the discovery of gold. They just did it. It's time we do the same.

Work Your Claim

When Samuel Brannan publicized the discovery of gold at Sutter's Mill in 1848 word spread quickly. (Fueled, in large part, by Brannan's own newspaper stories about the overnight fortunes being made in the hills.) The Gold Rush was on. Americans flocked to California because they were lured by an emotional desire to find their own gold.

The Gold Rush wasn't a lucky boom. It was a stroke of marketing genius. It is said that Mr. Brennan ran up and down the streets of San Francisco, shouting: *"Gold! Gold on the American River!"* Suddenly, the American River became the gold mining capital of the World.

Those early miners (called 49ers) found free land. Literally, free land. There was no private property. No tax structure. No licensing fees. Instead, any prospector could claim a piece of land as their own. Their claim was only valid as long as they actively worked their land. In an effort to mark their claim miners would pound wooden stakes in the ground. This came to be known as "staking their claim".

Like the 49ers, you need to stake your claim.

Not a physical claim. An emotional claim. A claim that defines your sense of place. A claim that paints a picture of what your neighborhood, town or city is. Like the 49ers, you need to work that claim if you want to keep it. You, and your town's future relies on it.

You need to carve out a sense of place and claim it as your own.

No Man's Land

As a 49er, evaluating how much gold your claim contained was your primary objective. The faster you worked your land the sooner you would know whether to keep your claim or find another one. Your claim is only valid as long as you are actively working the land. Abandoning your claim and staking a new chunk of land to work became part of a successful miner's strategy. Those abandoned claims became referred to as "no man's land".

Without a claim your neighborhood is stuck in limbo between what is and what could be.

You're in no man's land.

This is no man's land:

> "There are many reasons why INSERT CITY is a place where companies progress to the next level. Thanks to our prime geographic location, low cost of doing business, premier educational institutions, and diversified and highly trained workforce, INSERT CITY is one of the most attractive business communities today."

That is a quote lifted from a major metropolitan area's economic development website. What city would you insert? Boston? Phoenix? Dallas? Des Moines? Tampa? Your city? It doesn't matter. Positioning our towns as generic economic zones is not working. No business owner in their right mind would read that sentence or the entire website for that matter and decide to pick up their business, their family, and their employees and relocate. No one. We're marketing no man's land.

The problem is that we're trying to answer the wrong question. All of our marketing and positioning is focused on trying to answer the question: *"Why should I move to your town?"* We have to stop answering that question. Otherwise, you end up with generic gobbledygook that means nothing to everyone.

Stop trying to convince people to move to town. Instead, we should position our places so that people all over the world begin asking themselves: "Why shouldn't I move there?"

Where is the best place in the United States to build a winery? Napa Valley. Here's how Napa Valley positions itself: "Napa Valley is the premier wine-growing region in the world." They have staked their claim. Their claim invites any serious winemaker to ask themselves why they aren't in Napa Valley if they want to build their business. Napa Valley is known for something: winemaking. And they're constantly mining their claim ensuring that no one in the world can take away their simple position in the marketplace. And it works.

There's not much difference between Samuel Brannan running down the streets of San Francisco yelling, *"Gold! Gold! Gold on the American River"* and an imaginary Robert Mondavi running down the streets of Oakville, California, in 1965 yelling *"Wine! Wine! Wine in Napa Valley!"*

Stop trying to be everything to everyone and start being something to someone.

Stake Your Claim

It's time to redefine America one town at a time. It's time to resolve to be different. Resolve to be unique.

It's time for a grassroots revolution.

To make that happen, you must revolt against homogeneity. The more your town sounds like the city next door the less likely you are to grow, attract, and keep profitable businesses and the people they employ.

Revolt against doublespeak and development fads that promise to lure a new generation of business owners to your neighborhood. Stop looking for external support and start searching for local success.

Rally against marketing your city as a no man's land.

Instead, stake your claim. Make it simple. Make it visionary. Make it big!

Start by filling in the blanks: Your town is the _____ Capital of the World. Or, your town is America's _____ Capital. Like the 49ers before you, if someone is already actively mining that claim, find a new one. Your town is unique, and as Americans we celebrate the unique! We foster creativity and reward innovation. That's what made America great.

Find the existing success stories in your town. They're there, I promise. Find the tech start-up that's consciously decided to stay in your city because it's <u>not</u> Silicon Valley. Find the craft beer brewer who believes there's no better place to brew beer. Find the local manufacturer who's got the next big idea or the chef who's always trying something new. Maybe it's you and your business?

Embrace the idea that any business, no matter how small, can be the start of something big.

Bring back a bygone boom time. Not by happenstance or dumb luck, but by following a simple strategy. Your strategy will be deeply rooted in the accomplishments of the past but designed for the future.

Stake your claim.

About The Author

The Author, Andrew M. Davis. Photo Credit: Jon Davis

Andrew Davis is a world-renowned speaker and the best-selling author of
Brandscaping: Unleashing the Power of Partnerships.

Before co-founding and selling a digital marketing agency called
Tippingpoint Labs, Andrew wrote for Charles Kuralt, produced
for the Today Show, and worked for the Muppets.

Today, he's traveling the globe sharing his insight, experience,
stories, and optimistic ideals through his wildly fascinating
speaking engagements, guest lectures, and workshops.

For more information or to invite Andrew to speak in your city
or town visit <u>AKADrewDavis.com</u> or call 617.286.4009.

Acknowledgements

I have met thousands of wonderful people crisscrossing the United States. I have stopped at visitor's bureaus in the smallest of towns and the largest of cities. I have asked hundreds, maybe thousands, of people, what makes their town or city unique? To all of you, thank you. Thank you for taking my research seriously. Thank you for pointing me in the right direction. Thank you for taking the time to pull out a map and show me the way. I have high hopes for Town Inc. I believe this book. The simple idea it embodies can make any town a better place. But I couldn't have done it alone.

Without my editor, and self-publishing guide, Newt Barrett, and his wonderful wife, Maxine, this book would still be another audacious idea. Maxine and Newt have not wavered in their support and encouragement.

I have had the pleasure of sharing the stage with many great authors and talented public speakers, but Joe Pulizzi, Robert Rose, Jay Baer, and Ann Handley have made a tremendous contribution to this book. Their optimistic outlook, objective feedback, and constructive input are cherished more than they know.

I owe my wife a lifetime of gratitude. Elizabeth welcomes me home after every journey and she has supported my dreams at every turn. Her patience and belief in my ultimate success is as steadfast today as it was the day we married. Thank you.

My mother, Diana (a fellow author), taught me to think big and mentored me as a writer. My dad, Jan, encouraged me to see the world, meet the people, and to enjoy the journey. He motivated me to be the best at whatever I do—and I'm doing it. My father, Roy, has always believed in my ability to succeed even when he's had to put his own resources on the line. I appreciate the investments he and my stepmother, Betty, have made in my business and my education.

My brother, Jonathan (a professional photographer), took my press photos, but he's done much more than that—he's a creative inspiration to anyone who follows their passion. To my brother-in-law, Patrick, I owe a specific debt of gratitude. His persistent early morning calls from the West Coast prodding me to write the next best seller actually made me put my ass in the chair and write every day. To my brother-in-law, Ryan, thank you so much for taking the time to gather and document so much valuable research. Your inquisitive mind comes in handy. Thanks to everyone: all my friends and the rest of my extended family for your support. Especially, Katie and Luis Velez, Sean and Mistee Davis, Eric and Mallory Davis, Lindsey and Spencer King, and Kalie and Bob Austin.

I owe a special debt of gratitude to my former business partner, best man, and friend, James Cosco. If you and I hadn't made the trip to Alexandria, Indiana, to see the World's Largest Ball of Paint, this book and the ideas it contains might never have happened. To Bill Shander, whose data visualization expertise and longtime friendship is cherished.

To Paula Coony who introduced me to Professor Paul Fombelle, thank you. Professor Fombelle, your gracious offer to find a few enterprising and eager students to help quantify the value of a claim has been an unbelievably good experience. Matthew Gefen and Sahil Hundal, your work, your professional approach, your willingness to learn, and your slopegraphs are forever part of this book. Thank you for taking this project as seriously as you did.

To all of you who've embraced my creative spirit and inspired my thinking, thank you. This book is as much yours as it is mine.

CPSIA information can be obtained
at www.ICGtesting.com
Printed in the USA
FSOW02n1631180916
25084FS